Anna Claybo

100 MOST AWESOME THINGS ON THE PLANET

CONTENTS

Awesome
Human Creations 62

INTRODUCTION

The world we live in is a truly awesome place. Across its massive continents, deep oceans, and swirling skies are all kinds of fabulous places, amazing events, and astonishing sights. You'll get a little glimpse of many of them in this book.

NATURAL WONDERS

Although there are billions of humans on the planet, we're still just a tiny part of the natural world around us. We might feel in control, but the world is filled with fearsome forces that are much more powerful than we are – from giant creatures of the deep to heaving volcanoes, roaring waves, and weather that's wild, deadly, or plain weird. If this book makes you feel a bit small and helpless compared to the awesome power of the planet, that's because you are!

ALL OUR OWN WORK

We've achieved some pretty awesome stuff, too. Thanks to advances in human technology, we've built vast bridges, superfast speed machines, towering skyscrapers, perfect pyramids, and many other mind-boggling structures. Some of these mysterious monuments date from so far back in time, we don't even know how our awesome ancestors managed to make them – or why. Just think what people hundreds or thousands of years in the future might make of the things we build today!

WARNING!

A lot of the awesome things in this book are places you can go and visit – and there's nothing like seeing an erupting volcano, a giant waterfall, or a mysterious ruin with your own eyes. But if you do, remember that many awesome things can also be risky. Always stick to tourist trails, follow the advice of local guides, and obey safety signs and instructions.

ON THE PLANET—AND OFF THE PLANET!

This book also includes a few of the awesome wonders of space. Okay, so they're not strictly "on the planet" – but they're things we have spotted in our skies and can enjoy from our vantage point here on Earth. There are also a few amazing machines that we've sent into space ourselves.

The Lockheed SR-71 Blackbird, the fastest manned, air-breathing aircraft.

AWESOME RATING

😀	....	Cool!
😀 😀	....	Really cool!
😀 😀 😀	....	Totally amazing!
😀 😀 😀 😀	....	Incredible!
😀 😀 😀 😀 😀	.....	Completely awesome!

AWESOME NATURAL WONDERS

In this section you'll come face-to-face with the awesome forces and features of our natural world – from mighty tsunami waves, sky-high waterfalls, and exploding volcanoes to the world's most amazing cliffs, rivers and lakes, spooky caves, and deadly storms, and all the strange phenomena that fill our night sky. You'll also meet some of the world's most bizarre and beautiful living things, and encounter some incredible animal behaviour.

A gigantic wave about to wash away a car during a powerful storm in California.

MOUNT EVEREST

The jagged edges jutting into the air on Everest's slopes are awesomely dangerous.

You can't stand anywhere higher on the Earth than on the top of Mount Everest. The world's highest mountain is a massive, snow- and ice-topped chunk of rock in the Himalayas, a huge mountain range that lies in the middle of Asia.

BREATHTAKING

At 8,850 m (29,035 feet) high, Everest's peak is an awesome place to be. It's also icy cold, battered by hurricane-force winds, and the air contains less oxygen than it does at sea level. So, unless you have an oxygen mask, it's very hard to breathe up there.

CLIMBING EVEREST

In 1953, Sir Edmund Hillary and Tenzing Norgay were the first to reach the top of Everest and make it back home. Since then, another 3,000 people have managed it.

STILL RISING

The Himalayas were created when two landmasses, India and the rest of Asia, crashed into each other 50 million years ago, pushing the land up into a mountain range. The land is still moving, and so the Himalayas are still growing.

Climbing Everest is dangerous. You have to travel across steep ice slopes, use ladders to cross crevasses, and keep yourself warm.

DEADLY RIVAL

8,611 m (28,251 feet) tall, K2 in Pakistan and China is the second highest mountain in the world. It may be only the second tallest, but it is harder to climb. It's killed a quarter of those who've tried to climb it.

KILAUEA

How would you like to stand on the world's most active volcano? Well, actually, you can! It sounds scary, but because Kilauea, in Hawaii, is constantly erupting, it's safer than some other volcanoes. It usually releases its lava in a constant, gentle flow, instead of building it up until it bursts. But Kilauea is still pretty awesome!

ALWAYS ERUPTING

Kilauea is quite low for a mountain. It's a type of volcano known as a shield volcano. The lava that flows from it is runny and spreads out quickly, making the volcano wide and smooth. That makes it easier for tourists to visit the volcano and get quite close to the lava flows. It has several openings, or vents, where lava escapes. One of the vents, called Pu'u O'o, has been erupting non-stop since 1983. The lava usually streams downhill like a river, but it can also spit and splatter.

Red-hot lava flows from Kilauea Volcano, Hawaii.

INTO THE WAVES

Kilauea is close to the sea, and a lot of its lava flows down to the shore. There, the lava crackles and explodes as it plunges into the cold water, and cools superfast. Gradually, hardened lava from the volcano builds more and more new land in the water.

AWESOMENESS

It may not be the noisiest or most explosive volcano, but Kilauea lets you get up close to awesome real-life eruptions and lava flows.

This canyon is known around the world as one of our planet's most awesome sights.

GRAND CANYON

The Grand Canyon in Arizona certainly deserves the name "Grand". It's one of the biggest, most breathtaking rock formations you can see anywhere in the world.

The Grand Canyon is a gorge – a very deep, steep-sided river valley. The high cliffs on either side are striped in stunning shades of colour, made up of bands of rock of different types and ages.

Some gorges are narrow, but the Grand Canyon is very wide. It varies from 183 m to 30 km (600 feet to 19 miles) across. At its deepest, it's almost 2 km (1.25 miles) deep, and it reaches nearly 450 km (280 miles) in length.

HOW DID IT HAPPEN?

Gorges form when a river cuts through rock as it flows. Over millions of years, the River Colorado has carved its way down through the landscape to create the massive canyon. The river still flows along the bottom today.

DON'T LOOK DOWN

Nearly five million tourists visit the Grand Canyon area every year. You can take a plane or helicopter flight around it, or step out onto the Grand Canyon Skywalk, a glass-floored walkway 1,219 m (4,000 feet) above the bottom. Yikes!

The Grand Canyon, with the Colorado River flowing through it.

PULPIT ROCK

If you're scared of heights, just looking at this photo of Pulpit Rock (also called Preikestolen) is probably terrifying! This awesome natural rock formation stands about 600 m (2,000 feet) above Lysefjord, one of Norway's long, deep fjords, or sea inlets.

PICNIC TIME!

If you're brave enough, you could follow thousands of others along the steep trail up to Pulpit Rock for a day trip. In the summer, its flat, square platform is covered with visitors having picnics and enjoying the view. Leaning over the edge to peer at the 600-m (2,000 foot) drop is not a very good idea, but you can often see people lying on their stomachs to take a peek a little more safely.

AWESOMENESS

😵 😵 😵 😵

Pulpit Rock's stunning natural setting and spine-tingling awesomeness make it one of Norway's most famous natural attractions.

DON'T TRY THIS AT HOME!

Because it provides such a sheer vertical drop from an almost flat platform, Pulpit Rock is a popular spot for the extreme sport of BASE jumping. Jumpers leap off the platform with a parachute and try to sail safely down to the fjord below. But this is VERY dangerous, as winds can bash the jumpers against the rock on their way down. Ouch!

People enjoying the stunning view from Pulpit Rock.

CUT BY ICE

The fjords and cliffs were formed when glaciers flowed down from the mountains to the sea, cutting long, deep channels into the rock. When the ice melted, these valleys were filled by the sea.

CLIFFS OF KALAUPAPA

On the island of Molokai in Hawaii, towering over the tiny village of Kalaupapa, are some of the world's most enormous sea cliffs. Covered with tropical plants, the giant green cliffs plunge just over 1,000 m (3,280 feet) down to the sea.

STRAIGHT OR SLOPING?

There are many different types of cliffs. Some have a vertical drop, but many cliffs, like those of Kalaupapa, are more like extremely steep slopes. These cliffs are covered with thick green plant life, which is part of what makes them so strange and amazing to look at. There's even a hair-raising, winding path right on the cliff face, which you can travel down by mule.

VOLCANO LAND

All the islands of Hawaii were formed by volcanic eruptions from the sea, and these cliffs were originally part of a tall volcano. When part of the volcano fell away into the sea, the steep cliffs were left behind.

AWESOMENESS

These incredible cliffs are worth a trip all the way to Hawaii to see.

FAMOUS CLIFFS

Because the Kalaupapa cliffs look so otherworldly, they were used as part of the scenery for the movie *Jurassic Park*, which was about dinosaurs coming to life.

You can't reach Kalaupapa by car – only by boat, plane, mule, or on foot.

MOUNT THOR

If you think of a cliff as a purely vertical drop, then this is the world's biggest. The astonishing-looking Mount Thor stands on Baffin Island in the icy north of Canada. One side of it is a vast, overhanging cliff with a sheer 1,250-m (4,100 foot) drop.

CUT IN TWO

Mount Thor is made of a hard rock called granite. Its sheer shape was probably formed by ice freezing and thawing, which created cracks in the rock, causing part of it to fall away.

AWESOMENESS

😬 😬 😬 😬

Standing at the top of the world's biggest vertical drop must be completely MIND-BOGGLING!

BRAVE ATTEMPTS

Climbers first reached the top of Mount Thor in 1953. The mountain itself is 1,675 m (5,495 feet) above sea level. In 2006, another team decided to abseil down Mount Thor's cliff face – that is, to slide all the way down on a rope. They broke the record for the world's longest abseil.

Climbing thousands of metres on this sheer face is an epic experience.

Mount Thor and the frozen River Weasel.

DID YOU KNOW? If you dropped a pebble off the top of Mount Thor, it would take just under 16 seconds to hit the bottom.

MARIANA TRENCH

Most people know Mount Everest is the highest place on the planet – but what about the lowest? To go as deep as it's possible to go, you'd have to travel by deep-sea submarine to the very bottom of the Mariana Trench. This is a huge, deep channel on the floor of the Pacific Ocean, near Japan.

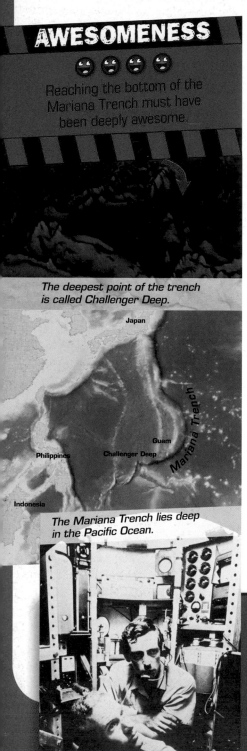

The deepest point of the trench is called Challenger Deep.

Japan

Mariana Trench

Guam

Challenger Deep

Philippines

Indonesia

The Mariana Trench lies deep in the Pacific Ocean.

CHALLENGER DEEP

Challenger Deep, the lowest point of the trench, lies 11,000 m (36,000 feet) below the sea surface. That's so deep that if you stood Mount Everest in the sea there, its peak would be covered by 2 km (1.33 miles) of water.

GOING DOWN

In 1960, explorers Jacques Piccard and Don Walsh reached the bottom in a diving vessel called the *Trieste*. The vessel had a very strong passenger chamber to keep the divers safe from the extreme water pressure in the deep ocean.

Piccard and Walsh in the Trieste.

WHAT DID THEY SEE?

Piccard and Walsh didn't know if any creatures lived so deep down in the sea. But when they landed and looked out of their window, they saw a flatfish on the muddy seabed and a shrimp.

HYDROTHERMAL VENTS

The bottom of the sea isn't just deep – it's also strange, with creatures and features unlike anything on land. Among the most awesome sights are hydrothermal vents, where really hot water spurts out of the ocean floor.

DEEP-SEA DISCOVERY

Scientists first found hydrothermal vents in 1977. They used deep-sea diving machines to investigate why some parts of the sea contained extra-warm water. They found that the water flows into cracks in the seabed, where it is heated by hot volcanic rocks. Then, the superheated water pours back out through holes called hydrothermal vents.

CRAZY CREATURES

Hydrothermal vents are home to some crazy-looking creatures, such as giant tube worms. These weird white worms can grow up to 3 m (10 feet) long! Instead of eating, they have special bacteria in their bodies. The bacteria trap chemicals from the hot vent water and turn them into food for the tube worm.

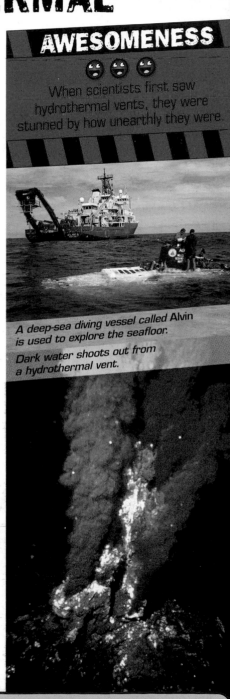

A deep-sea diving vessel called Alvin is used to explore the seafloor.

Dark water shoots out from a hydrothermal vent.

BLACK SMOKERS At some vents, the water contains dissolved minerals. The minerals around the vent can build up into chimneys; some are up to 60 m (200 feet) tall. The minerals often make the water dark, so the chimneys are called black smokers.

OX BEL HA CAVE

Exploring underground caves is challenging – but it's even harder when they're completely full of water! These caves are beneath land, not in the sea, but when you go down into them you find yourself in a kind of underground river instead of a dry tunnel. The Ox Bel Ha cave system, in Mexico, is the daddy of them all.

AWESOMENESS

It must be incredible to swim through the watery caves, discovering new rooms, tunnels, and connections.

EXPLORING OX BEL HA

Divers only began exploring Ox Bel Ha properly in 1998. They entered it through sea caves and by diving down through cave pools called cenotes. They discovered more and more branching tunnels and chambers, leading far under the Mexican jungle. Some are filled with awesome rock pillars, ridges, needles, and other rock formations. Where the tunnel passes under a cenote that is open to the air, you can look up and see fish swimming in the sunlight above you.

You'll need breathing equipment to enjoy the wonders of these caves.

RACE FOR THE RECORD

Ox Bel Ha cave and another cave system, Sac Actun, are among the world's biggest underwater cave systems. Divers are hoping to find a link between Sac Actun and another cave, Dos Ojos, which would give it the record.

The name Ha Long Bay means "bay of the descending dragon".

HA LONG BAY

Though you may have never been to this breathtaking, beautiful bay in Vietnam, you may recognize it from movies and advertisements. Its calm, mirror-like waters are dotted with more than 1,600 rocky mini-islands, pillars, and towers. Some are covered with lush greenery and are home to all kinds of tropical wildlife.

LIMESTONE LUMPS
Ha Long Bay's islands have taken millions of years to form from limestone that's been shifted, shoved, worn, and dissolved by water and the movements of the Earth. Some of the towers are up to 200 m (656 feet) tall, as tall as skyscrapers. Others are hollow lumps with huge, dark caves inside.

AWESOMENESS

If you're ever in Vietnam, don't miss out on this amazing place!

COME AND EXPLORE
Ha Long Bay is one of Vietnam's top tourist attractions. Few humans live on the islands now, but ancient tools have been found in some of the caves, showing that early peoples used them as homes.

Many people take boats to the islands to explore.

DRAGON SPIT According to legend, the bay was formed when dragons spat out jewels, which turned into rocky islands. They stopped ships from landing and protected Vietnam from its enemies.

AWESOMENESS

This awesome reef is the biggest thing on our planet that's been built by living things.

GREAT BARRIER REEF

The Great Barrier Reef is the world's biggest coral reef. It's HUGE. It stretches for more than 2,000 km (1,250 miles) along the coast of Australia, forming a chain of coral islands and underwater platforms that can be seen from space.

COOL CORAL

Coral is a kind of skeleton, made by tiny sea creatures called coral polyps, which are a bit like sea anemones. Each polyp builds a skeleton around itself using sea minerals. Each generation builds more coral on top of the old coral, and gradually a big structure, or reef, builds up. There are many different species of coral polyps.

UNDERWATER WONDERLAND

While some coral reefs become islands, others are still underwater, where they provide a habitat, or home, for all kinds of sea creatures.

The Great Barrier Reef is a spectacular place to be.

REEF WILDLIFE

Besides the beautiful coral itself, divers at the Great Barrier Reef can see turtles, octopuses, sea snakes, jellyfish, dolphins, and more than 1,000 fish species, including more than 100 types of sharks and rays.

A scuba diver observes some of the coral of the Great Barrier Reef.

WILDLIFE WATCH
Polyps provide food for some creatures, while coral caves and formations give others places to hide or lay their eggs. So the Great Barrier Reef is a top destination for scuba diving and wildlife-watching.

GREAT BLUE HOLE

AWESOMENESS

There are other blue holes, but this is the biggest and most impressive.

As you can see in the picture, this awesome natural formation is exactly what it sounds like — a huge, deep hole in the seabed. It appears dark blue because it's so much deeper than the surrounding shallow water. The hole, off the coast of Belize in Central America, measures over 300 m (1,000 feet) across and 125 m (412 feet) deep.

MYSTERIOUS HOLE

The Great Blue Hole is so perfectly round, it looks as if humans might have made it. It is believed to have formed long ago when this part of the sea was dry land. The hole used to be an enormous underground cave, covered by a rocky roof. When the last ice age ended around 10,000 years ago and sea levels rose, the roof collapsed and seawater filled the hole.

WHAT'S IN THE HOLE?

The water deep in the hole is clear and still, and doesn't have much oxygen mixed in with it, so not many sea creatures live there. But fish, shrimp, and some large sharks, such as bull sharks, often swim near the surface. Deep down on the hole's vertical walls are awesome stalactites and other rock formations, which probably formed when the hole was a dry cave.

DIVING HEAVEN

The great ocean expert Jacques Cousteau said the Great Blue Hole was one of the best places in the world to go diving. He explored and made underwater films of it. Many divers still go there now to explore it.

AWESOMENESS

😆 😆 😆 😆

Deep, strange, and unique, this has to be the world's most incredible lake.

LAKE BAIKAL

Lake Baikal in Siberia, Russia, is the deepest and the oldest lake in the world. It contains a staggering 20 per cent of the world's fresh flowing water. Pretty impressive!

DEEP AND DARK

Baikal isn't the world's biggest lake by surface area, but it's so deep that it holds more water than any other lake – 23,000 cubic km (5,500 cubic miles) in total. If Baikal was empty, and all the rivers in the world flowed into it, it would take nearly a year to fill up. At its deepest, it's almost 1,620 m (5,315 feet) deep. No sunlight can reach down to those murky depths, so the bottom of the lake is pitch-black.

UNIQUE BEASTS

Living in Lake Baikal are more than 1,000 species of wildlife that aren't found anywhere else – including the Baikal seal, or nerpa. The nerpa loves to feed on an awesomely freaky type of fish called the golomyanka, also found only in Lake Baikal. These fish are almost transparent, and their bodies are full of a type of oil. If they're caught and put in sunlight, they dissolve, leaving just a pile of goopy oil and bones. Weird!

A horse and rider on the frozen Lake Baikal, in the movie Serko.

DID YOU KNOW? Siberia is so cold that Baikal freezes every winter. The ice is so thick that people drive their snowmobiles over it to go fishing.

ANTARCTIC ICE SHEET

At the southernmost end of our planet, lying over most of Antarctica, is the biggest mass of ice anywhere in the world. The Antarctic ice sheet is a giant glacier or ice cap that covers an area as big as the United States and Europe put together. In parts, it's more than 4 km (2.5 miles) deep, and it contains 80 per cent of the world's fresh water.

ANCIENT ICE

Most of Antarctica's ice starts off as snowfall. It's too cold in Antarctica for the snow to melt, so instead it just gets compressed into ice by more snow falling on top of it.

TIME TRAVEL

We can use the Antarctic ice to look back in time! Tiny air bubbles trapped in it reveal what the atmosphere on Earth was like long ago. Scientists drill long cylinders of ice, called ice cores, out of the ice sheet so they can study these air bubbles.

ICEBERG MACHINE

As the ice builds up and gets heavier, it gradually slips and flows downhill towards the coast around Antarctica. It pushes out over the sea, forming an ice shelf. Every so often, part of the ice shelf breaks off, forming an iceberg that floats out to sea.

AWESOMENESS

It's freezing, unimaginably enormous, and lets us look back in time – the Antarctic ice sheet is truly awesome.

DID YOU KNOW? The Antarctic ice sheet is so huge that it completely covers several large mountains. Scientists detected the mountains through the ice.

UYUNI SALT FLAT

Two vehicles cross the amazingly vast Uyuni Salt Flat of Bolivia.

It's a **STUNNING** sight — the bright blue sky and white clouds reflected in a brilliantly clear 'mirror'. This amazing vision is something you can sometimes see at the Uyuni Salt Flat in Bolivia, the biggest salt flat in the world. It has an area of 10,582 square km (4,085 square miles) and lies 3,656 m (11,995 feet) above sea level, up in the Andes mountains.

AWESOMENESS

A giant white salt flat is an astonishing sight to take in – a bit like being on the Moon.

WHAT'S A SALT FLAT?

A salt flat, or salt lake, is like a normal lake, but instead of being made of water, it's a completely flat stretch of hard, solid salt. Salt flats form when salt and other minerals collect in a lake and the water then dries up, leaving the salt behind. Many salt flats are mainly dry, but receive a thin layer of rainwater for part of the year. At Uyuni, this water is what turns the salt flat into a vast, shimmering mirror.

USEFUL UYUNI

You may think it is empty and barren, but, in fact, this is a busy place. It's a breeding ground for flamingos, and other animals, such as foxes and rodents, live on rocky 'islands' sticking up out of the salt. Since it's flat, it makes a good route for travellers across the Andes, and thousands go there every year. In addition, scientists use the flat surface to help them test and program Earth-measuring satellites.

SALT HOTELS

As a particular regional attraction, locals have built several salt hotels to provide accomodation for tourists, using blocks of salt from the lake as building materials.

DEAD SEA

The Dead Sea isn't a sea, but an extremely salty, low-lying lake, between the hot desert lands of Israel and Jordan. It's called the Dead Sea because it's so salty that wildlife can't live in it. It's awesomely weird in many ways.

SUPERLOW LAKE

Most lakes have rivers running into them, and then out again down to the sea. But at the Dead Sea, this can't happen because the Dead Sea itself is much lower than the sea. Its shores are around 400 m (1,300 feet) lower than sea level, making them the lowest-lying areas of land on Earth.

A man and boy smother themselves in Dead Sea mud.

MAGIC WATER

As water can't flow out, it evaporates in the hot sunshine, and the salt and minerals in it are left behind. Over time, the salt and minerals become more and more concentrated, so the Dead Sea is now almost 30 per cent salt (while normal seawater is about 3 per cent salt). This makes the water very dense.

Because the water is so dense in the Dead Sea, you float much higher.

DID YOU KNOW? Lots of people with skin diseases visit the Dead Sea. The salt and minerals in the water, and in the mud on the shore, often seem to make sore skin better.

AMAZON RIVER

The River Amazon in South America is the largest river in the world. Though it is not as long as the River Nile in Africa, it is by far the widest river, and holds an awesome amount of water.

WATER WORLD

Where it flows into the Atlantic Ocean, the two banks of the Amazon River are 190 km (120 miles) apart. A speedboat travelling across the river at 97 km/h (60 mph) would take two hours to reach the other side! The river stretches more than 6,400 km (4,000 miles), from deep in the Amazon rainforest all the way to the coast. Every single second, about a day's worth of drinking water for 100 million people pours out of the river into the Atlantic Ocean!

A stunning view of the curving River Amazon and the forest around it.

AWESOMENESS

Holding 20 per cent of the world's water, this is one awesome waterway.

A variety of wildlife can be seen in the River Amazon, such as this bull shark.

WHAT, NO BRIDGE? Most of the world's big rivers have big bridges over them – but not the Amazon. Because it's mainly surrounded by rainforest, there aren't many major roads leading across it. If you need to cross the river or travel up it, you have to take a boat.

OKAVANGO DELTA

You may think that all rivers lead to the sea, but this is not true. The River Okavango in Africa is a very big river, but it never reaches the sea. Instead, it flows into a huge delta, in the middle of the Kalahari Desert.

AWESOMENESS

If you like wildlife, this is one of the most spectacular places in the world to visit.

DISAPPEARING WATER

As the River Okavango flows into the delta and spreads out, some of the water evaporates into the hot air. The rest is mostly sucked up by plants and escapes from their leaves, or is drunk by animals. Every year from May to October, the river floods and brings extra water to the delta, creating a wet season. At other times of year the delta is much drier.

DELTA SAFARI

The Okavango Delta is famous for its stunning natural beauty and amazing wildlife. When it floods, thirsty animals from a huge surrounding area travel there in search of drinking water. If you take a boat through the calm waterways, you can see elephants, antelope, zebras, lions, leopards, rare birds, and colourful insects, while hippos and crocodiles lurk beneath the surface.

African elephants wade through a swamp in the Okavango Delta.

WHAT'S A DELTA? A delta
is a place where a river spreads out and splits into lots of separate channels, with many islands and mud banks in between.

The Okavango Delta from space.

ANGEL FALLS

Imagine floating or canoeing along a river — then suddenly shooting out into the sky! That's what happens in Venezuela, at Angel Falls, the world's tallest waterfall.

CLIFF DROP

Angel Falls flows over an amazingly tall cliff on one side of a tepui, a high, narrow, flat-topped mountain, which is a typical feature of the Venezuelan landscape. From the top, the water drops straight down in a shimmering, misty column. In total, including some additional rocky falls at the bottom, the waterfall is 979 m (3,212 feet) high — taller than the world's highest skyscraper.

ANGELS AND DEVILS

Angel Falls is white, misty, and looks magical, but that's not why it got its name. It's actually named after James Angel, a pilot who flew his plane around and over the falls in 1935 and reported them to the outside world. In the local language, the tepui the falls flow over is actually called Auyán-tepuí, or "Devil Mountain".

AWESOMENESS

You'll never forget this sight — especially if you take a flight around the falls.

DID YOU KNOW? A lot of the water that goes over Angel Falls never reaches the bottom! As it drops, the wind turns it into spray or water vapour and carries it away.

IGUAÇU FALLS

AWESOMENESS

😨 😨

Thousands of tourists flock to see these fabulous falls every year.

While Angel Falls is awesomely high, delicate, and beautiful, Iguaçu Falls is awesomely wide and LOUD. It's the world's biggest set of falls, with the most water flowing over it, and you can hear its thundering, watery roar from many kilometres away.

FULL FLOOD

It may be less than a tenth of the height of Angel Falls, the world's highest waterfall, but what Iguaçu lacks in height, it makes up for in volume. About 1,756 cubic m (62,000 cubic feet) of water gushes over this huge drop every second, though this varies a lot.

HUGE HORSESHOE

Like many big waterfalls, Iguaçu flows over a giant horseshoe-shaped cliff, with the water splitting into many different minifalls, or cascades. The whole of the falls covers about 2.7 km (1.5 miles), and the biggest single cataract, or large waterfall, called the "Devil's Throat", is 150 m (492 feet) wide. The falls are on the River Iguaçu, on the border between Brazil and Argentina.

DID YOU KNOW? You may have heard of two other great waterfalls, Niagara Falls in North America and Victoria Falls in Africa. Both are among the world's biggest and are well worth a trip to see – though they are not quite as impressive as the amazing Iguaçu.

ATACAMA DESERT

The Atacama is dry. *Really* dry. It's so incredibly dry that in parts of it, experts think it may have never rained at all. It's the world's driest desert and is close to the coast of Chile, in South America.

WHY SO DRY?

The Atacama has mountains on both sides of it – the Andes on one side, and the Chilean coastal range on the other. When rain clouds come along, they rise up the mountains, cool, condense, and drop their rain before reaching the top. So clouds rarely reach the Atacama, lying in the middle.

LIFELESS LANDSCAPE

Because of this, the Atacama is pretty barren. Many deserts have scrubby plants or cacti, and tough animals such as rattlesnakes and camels that can go without much to drink. But in large parts of the Atacama, there's nothing. Near the coast, however, fog from the sea provides enough water for mesquite and cacti. And in the middle of the desert, there's even a town, San Pedro de Atacama. Its water supply comes from underground springs that carry water in from other areas.

AWESOMENESS

The Atacama is one of the most unearthly places on the planet, where you can experience complete silence.

Rock formations in the Atacama Desert.

DID YOU KNOW?

With its vast areas of reddish sands devoid of any trees, plants, or wildlife, much of the Atacama looks like the surface of the planet Mars! So it's often been used to film scenes of Mars for science-fiction movies.

NAMIB DESERT

The Namib in Africa is thought to be the oldest desert on the planet – it's been dry as a bone for around 55 million years. It's also one of the world's most strange and beautiful places, with its soaring sand dunes and the spooky Skeleton Coast.

DESERT DUNES

If you see a classic photo of a pointy, red-brown sand dune, with an oryx, or desert antelope, trekking across it, it was probably taken in the Namib Desert. The dunes form when wind blows across the desert, piling the dry sand up into heaps. As the sand shifts and rolls down one side of the dune, it leaves a razor-like ridge along the top.

THE SKELETON COAST

Next to the Namib Desert is the Skeleton Coast, a stretch of deadly, foggy desert coastline that sailors used to call 'The Gates of Hell'. Hundreds of ships have been wrecked here, after being lost in the fog and run aground. Over time, sand is blown into the sea and makes more land, so the wrecks can be found lying on the shore far from any waves.

The stunning red sand dunes of Sossusvlei, in the Namib Desert.

AWESOMENESS

😲 😲 😲

An awesomely eerie desert where you could easily get lost forever!

WEIRD WILDLIFE Some curious creatures live here. The sidewinder snake skips sideways across the ground to keep as much of its body as possible off the hot sand. The Namib desert beetle lets water droplets from fog collect on its body, then lifts its bottom to tip the water into its mouth.

CAVE OF CRYSTALS

In the year 2000, miners were searching for lead and silver 300 m (1,000 feet) below ground in Mexico's Naica Mine. Instead, they were amazed to find a natural cave filled with giant crystals. It's now known as the Cueva de los Cristales, or Cave of Crystals.

WHAT ARE CRYSTALS?

Crystals are natural formations made by certain types of minerals. Depending on the shape of the mineral molecules, they often grow into regular, geometric shapes, such as cubes or many-sided columns. This usually happens when minerals are dissolved in water, then gradually build up into solid shapes.

GIANT GYPSUM

The Cave of Crystals was filled with water until the owners of the mine unknowingly drained the cave. Its crystals are made of a mineral called gypsum, and are among the biggest crystals on earth – they are awesomely gigantic. The biggest is about 11 m (36 feet) long – as big as some buildings!

Explorers surrounded by giant crystals in the Cave of Crystals.

AWESOMENESS

There's no other cave quite like this known on the planet.

CRYSTAL HOT! The crystals look icy, but in fact the Cave of Crystals is swelteringly hot. Being deep underground and warmed by volcanic rocks, its temperature is more than 40°C (110°F).

AWESOMENESS

The cave is so mind-blowing that one of its discoverers panicked when he couldn't work out where he was!

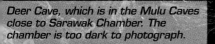

Deer Cave, which is in the Mulu Caves close to Sarawak Chamber. The chamber is too dark to photograph.

SARAWAK CHAMBER

Most underground caves are narrow, winding tunnels with a few bigger chambers here and there. But the Sarawak Chamber in Malaysia is massive. It's the world's biggest natural cave chamber and is so vast, it's like a huge cathedral, stadium, or concert hall underground.

MIND-BOGGLINGLY BIG

The chamber measures roughly 700 m (2,300 feet) long, 400 m (1,300 feet) across, and 70 m (230 feet) high. Its floor is steep, bumpy, and covered in rock formations and boulders. If it was

BAT HEAVEN The Sarawak Chamber is part of the Mulu limestone cave system, which also contains many other chambers and tunnels. One passageway, Deer Cave, is home to well over a million bats.

flat, you could park 45 Airbus A380 jumbo jets (the world's biggest airliner) inside.

DRAMATIC DISCOVERY

Local people may have already known about the chamber, but outsiders first found it in 1981. Three English cavers were exploring the Mulu cave system when they found it. It was so big, they couldn't see the sides — they just knew from the echoes it made that it was enormous. Since then, the cave has been measured.

MAMMOTH CAVE

AWESOMENESS

You could explore these caves for years. Cavers are still finding new parts.

Under the state of Kentucky lies Mammoth Cave, the longest cave tunnel system anywhere on Earth. It has 580 km (360 miles) of passageways, all linked together.

BIG, BUT NOT WOOLLY

Many people think that Mammoth Cave got its name because woolly mammoths used to live in it, or because their fossils were found there. In fact there's no sign of any woolly mammoth activity – the cave just got its name because 'mammoth' means 'very big'.

DECORATIONS

The tunnels and chambers are filled with amazing "decorations" – the name cavers give to beautiful, intricate rock formations.

CAVE CREATURES

Many parts of the cave have underground rivers and pools. In them live several species of 'troglobites' – creatures that spend their whole lives in caves.

Cavers in the massive Mammoth Cave.

wworms on the cave ceiling
emble stars in the night sky.

DID YOU KNOW?
Glowworms glow in order to
lure prey, such as tiny passing
flies.

GLOWWORM CAVE

**Glowworm Cave, part of the Waitomo cave system in New Zealand,
isn't the world's biggest, longest, or most dramatic cave – but it
offers a uniquely awesome experience.**

SEEING THE CAVE
When you visit the cave, you climb
down through three underground
chambers to a river, which you
travel along by boat. The roof is
lit up by thousands of glowing fly
maggots, or glowworms, dangling
from the cave ceiling.

DISCOVERY
The cave was first fully explored
in the 1880s by a local Maori
chief, Tane Tinorau, and an
English explorer, Fred Mace.
Tane Tinorau found the upper
entrance to the cave and began
taking tourists to view it.

LAVA

We think of rocks as cold and hard. Yet in thousands of places around the world, you can see what rocks look like when they're heated so much that they melt into eyeball-scorchingly hot lava.

INSIDE THE EARTH

Deep below the surface, our planet is so hot that the rock there is mostly a thick, molten liquid called magma. In some parts of the planet, it can escape through weak spots and cracks in the crust. Once it emerges into the air, it's called lava.

Scorching hot lava flows from Kilauea Volcano in Hawaii.

MAKING A VOLCANO

As lava escapes from the Earth, it cools and hardens into solid rock. This is how volcanoes form – the lava spouts out of a hole, hardens, and becomes a mountainous heap. Whenever the volcano erupts, more lava flows out of the top and down the sides.

DID YOU KNOW?

When flowing lava hits trees and bushes, they often crackle and pop as the water inside them boils. It's incredible!

ON THE BRIDGE Volcanologists (volcano scientists) often study lava up close. They sometimes stand where a crust of cooled, solid lava covers a lava flow that's still melted and moving. It's very dangerous!

PYROCLASTIC FLOW

Any volcanic eruption is pretty impressive, but you'd never forget seeing a pyroclastic flow. It's a torrent of rocks and glowing hot, deadly gas that bursts out of some types of volcanoes when they erupt.

ROCK RIVER

Pyroclastic flows happen when a lot of pressure builds up inside a volcano. Then – BANG! – it explodes, and gas, lava, shattered rocks, ash, and dust burst out. Mixed together, they behave like a liquid, so the flow zooms down the mountainside like a river. Pyroclastic flows can travel as fast as 100 km/h (60 mph), and have a temperature of up to 700°C (1,300°F).

MAKE YOUR ESCAPE!

When pyroclastic flows land on towns or villages, the rocks crush everything flat, while the hot dust and gases choke and burn anyone around. If you're lucky, you could avoid one by running uphill.

The volcano on the Caribbean island of Montserrat exploded violently and unexpectedly in January 2009.

AWESOMENESS

😀 😀 😀 😀

A pyroclastic flow is an awesomely scary sight. Just make sure you live to tell the tale!

DEADLY FLOWS

In 1991, 43 people died in a pyroclastic flow while visiting Mount Unzen in Japan. In 1902, a pyroclastic flow from Mount Pelée in the Caribbean swamped the town of Saint-Pierre, killing 29,000 people. The ruins at Pompeii are also the result of a pyroclastic flow (see page 75).

YELLOWSTONE

Satellite image of the caldera.

West Thumb Geyser Basin, in Yellowstone National Park.

One of the biggest volcanoes in the world isn't a mountain — it's a wide, flat bowl shape, or caldera. It's the Yellowstone caldera, in Wyoming.

AWESOMENESS

Yellowstone is an incredible place, but you wouldn't want to be there if it blew up in a massive eruption!

EARTH-DESTROYING POWER

Yellowstone is a supervolcano — a volcano so enormous and powerful that when it erupts, instead of forming a pointy peak, it blasts away a giant crater in the Earth.

DID YOU KNOW?

Some scientists think that Yellowstone is due for another supervolcanic eruption soon. If it was an eruption like the one 630,000 years ago, it would be the biggest in human history. It could throw out enough rock and ash to cover most of the United States in a thick layer of dust, and darken the sky around the world for years.

Yellowstone's last giant eruption was about 630,000 years ago. It left a huge oval crater around 50 km (28 miles) across and 80 km (47 miles) long.

WAITING TO HAPPEN

Today, Yellowstone is filled with forests and wildlife. It also has hot springs, squirting geysers, and fumaroles, where hot gas escapes from the ground. The area around the caldera is a national park, where tourists visit. But just under the surface is a vast chamber of molten magma and gas that could one day cause another eruption.

OLD FAITHFUL

Old Faithful Geyser is one of the most famous of the volcanic features found in Yellowstone National Park. It's a geyser that shoots out a jet of boiling hot water several times a day – usually about once every 90 minutes.

STEAMY STUFF

Geysers are found in volcanic areas where hot magma heats rocks under the ground. If there's a space or chamber under the ground, water can collect there, and the hot rocks make it boil. This pressure builds up until the water erupts (a bit like a volcano erupting lava) and shoots out. Unlike lava, though, the water then sinks back down the hole, and the whole cycle starts again.

GIANT FOUNTAIN

Old Faithful is especially awesome because it's unusually big and goes off so often. When it's not erupting, it's just a hole in the ground. But when it goes off, it can squirt scalding hot water 52 m (170 feet) up in the sky – as high as a 20-storey city building.

Boiling hot water shoots out from Old Faithful.

DID YOU KNOW?

According to local tales, people used to throw their laundry into Old Faithful to wash it. The eruption would then fling it out to be collected.

AWESOMENESS

If you get the chance, it's mind-blowing to see a geyser erupting – especially this one.

AMAZON RAIN FOREST

The Amazon rainforest is the world's biggest rainforest. It covers about 6 million square km (2 million square miles) of South America, all around the mighty River Amazon.

REALLY RAINY

Rainforests are incredibly wet! They're found near the equator, where it's very hot. Every morning, the Sun's heat makes water evaporate from the ground, from rivers and from the plants in the forest, forming clouds. Then, every afternoon, the clouds drop their rain in heavy showers.

WILD WORLD

The Amazon rainforest is PACKED with wildlife. If you took a stroll through it, you'd be close to monkeys, tropical birds, countless tree frogs, lizards and snakes, millions of ants, spiders, other creepy-crawlies, and thousands of fish and fungi, not to mention all the trees.

Huge trees with massive trunks can be found in the Amazon.

GOING, GOING, GONE?

Every year, a large area of the Amazon rainforest is cut down to make space for farmland. If this continues, the area covered by the rainforest could be reduced by up to a half within a few decades.

SUNDARBANS

Everyone's heard of the rainforest, but not so many know about mangrove forests – a stranger, swampier, and much saltier type of forest, found on coasts. The Sundarbans is the world's most spectacular and important mangrove forest.

AWESOMENESS

If you ever get a chance to go there, you'll be amazed by this mysterious, magical, and dangerous swampland.

SUPER SWAMP
The Sundarbans lie where the great River Ganges meets the sea, on the border between India and Bangladesh. Here, the river spreads out into a delta of thousands of muddy, swampy channels, mud banks, and islands.

Unlike most trees, the mangroves grow right next to the sea. When the tide comes in, it covers their stems and roots with salty water.

CREATURES OF THE SUNDARBANS
All this makes an awesome habitat for wildlife – from deadly venomous snakes and killer crocodiles and sharks, to beautiful waterbirds, fish, insects, and deer, and, most famous of all, the highly endangered Bengal tiger.

TERRIBLE TIGERS
Tigers don't normally eat humans, but in the Sundarbans, they've developed a taste for human flesh. Several people get eaten alive every year.

A tiger gets wet in a river in the Sundarbans.

AWESOMENESS

😵 😵 😵 😵 😵

How can such a small, delicate creature fly so far, and find its way to the exact place where its great-great-grandparents hibernated?

Hundreds of monarch butterflies on a tree trunk in Mexico.

MONARCH MIGRATIONS

The journeys of monarch butterflies are incredible. Not only do they migrate, or travel, a vast distance — they also know exactly where they're going, though they've never been there before!

WHAT HAPPENS?

Every spring, monarch caterpillars hatch from their eggs, feed, grow, and make a cocoon, then emerge as beautiful butterflies. Then those butterflies lay eggs and have babies. Then those babies grow up and have babies, and so do their babies.

By now, it's the fall. The fourth set of butterflies are different from the others and live much longer. Instead of laying eggs and dying, they fly south to spend the winter somewhere warmer. Monarchs from Canada, for example, fly thousands of kilometres to Mexico. In the spring, they mate, then fly back north to lay their eggs, and the cycle starts again.

THE RIGHT TREE

Each monarch follows the same route its ancestor took — sometimes even returning to the same tree. How do they know where to go? Scientists think the information must be somehow stored in their bodies, but they're still trying to work it out.

YUCK! Monarchs lay their eggs on the poisonous milkweed plant, and the caterpillars feed on it. The poison stays in their bodies when they are adults, making them dangerous for other animals to eat. This helps monarchs avoid being eaten by predators.

Male emperor penguins gather together and keep the eggs safe.

EMPEROR PENGUIN MARCH

For emperors, the planet's biggest penguins, having babies is hard work. They have to trek for weeks, go without food, and almost freeze to death!

OFF WE GO!
Emperor penguins live around the coast of Antarctica – but they waddle many kilometres inland to breed safely. Each female lays one egg. There are no fish nearby, so the mother leaves the father to keep the egg warm, by balancing it on his feet and covering it with his stomach, while she trudges back to the sea for food.

BRRRRRRR!
The male penguins huddle together with nothing to eat! They use up their body fat to stay alive. Two months later, the eggs hatch and the females return. They cough up fishy food from their stomachs for the chicks. Then it's the males' turn to trek back to the sea for dinner.

AWESOMENESS

Imagine your parents had to go through all this just to get you fish for dinner!

DEVOTED DADS Emperor penguin fathers aren't the only ones to care for their babies. Male Siamese fighting fish keep their eggs safe in a nest made of bubbles. And male seahorses even get pregnant! They hold their eggs in a pouch on their stomachs.

MASAI MARA

A crocodile snaps at a passing wildebeest with its fearsome jaws.

If you want to see big cats chasing and pouncing on gazelles and zebras, or wildebeests thundering across the plains, the Masai Mara is the place to go. It's Africa's most famous safari park, with an amazing array of rare and beautiful wildlife and natural sights.

WHO LIVES HERE?

The Masai Mara is in Kenya, East Africa, and it's mostly made up of grassland with some swamps, rivers, and scattered trees and rocks. It's home to all kinds of awesome creatures – lions, cheetahs and leopards, rhinos, crocodiles, zebras, giraffes, elephants, ostriches, and vultures.

MASS MIGRATION

Every year around June–July, zebras, wildebeests, and gazelles migrate, or travel, from the Serengeti plains in the south to the Masai Mara, where they can find more water and fresh grass. Around two million animals make the 1,600-km (1,000 mile) round-trip, crossing plains and rivers where predators lie in wait to feast on them.

AWESOMENESS

Around 200,000 tourists visit the Masai Mara every year to see some of the most awesome wildlife on the planet in action.

LOCUST STORMS

Imagine a swarm of big, flapping, hungry insects so huge and thick that it blocks out the sunlight and fills the air around you! There are locusts crawling in your face and clothes – aaarrrgh! But they don't want to eat you. They're in search of plants to gobble.

WHAT IS A LOCUST?

Locusts are basically large grasshoppers, found mainly in Africa and Asia. They're known as locusts when they flock together into massive swarms, known as locust 'storms'. Experts think this happens when there's lots of rain and a good food supply. The grasshoppers, which are normally brown or green, become red, yellow, or black and yellow, and set off in big groups on feeding frenzies.

AWESOMENESS

The sheer number of creatures in a swarm makes this one of the most incredible sights on the planet.

YUM! One way to get something good out of a locust attack is to catch and eat them. They make a very healthy, high-protein food and they taste good, too.

OH NO! MY CROPS!

A locust storm is extremely bad news for farmers. When locusts arrive, they can consume fields of rice, maize, and other cereal crops in minutes. They'll also devour all kinds of leaves, fruit, and vegetables. They can cause famines by leaving large areas of land with no crops at all.

DID YOU KNOW?

A single locust swarm can be 1,200 sq km (460 square miles) and can contain 100 BILLION locusts. That's more locusts than there are people on Earth!

A swarm of locusts on a beach in Fuerteventura, one of the Canary Islands.

BLUE WHALE

A blue whale isn't just big. It's AWESOMELY big. It's not only the biggest animal on our planet, it's also the biggest animal that has ever lived – bigger than any dinosaur. Its heart is the size of a small car, and some of its blood vessels are so wide that you could fit inside them!

AWESOMENESS

😝 😝 😝 😝 😝

This has to be the world's most amazing animal.

Blue whales can sometimes be seen leaping out of the water.

ASTONISHINGLY BIG

A blue whale can grow to almost 30 m (100 feet) long (about as long as four classrooms in a row) and can weigh 181 tonnes (200 tons). Some dinosaurs were longer, with their snake-like necks and tapering tails – but they weighed much less, at probably only 90 tonnes (100 tons). Blue whales are a massive, long, solid cylinder shape, so they're much heavier.

SCARY MONSTERS?

Though they're giants, blue whales don't pose a threat to humans. They're not fierce hunters – they simply cruise through the world's oceans with their mouths wide open, scooping up lots of small shrimp and tiny fish to eat.

A blue whale's head is about one quarter of its body length, making it one of the biggest heads on Earth.

SINGING GIANTS As well as being the biggest, blue whales are among the loudest creatures on Earth. They sing a grunting, moaning song. They use their voices to find a mate, and can hear one another hundreds of kilometres apart.

CALIFORNIA REDWOOD

The tallest living thing on Earth stands up to 70 times taller than an average human. The California redwood, or coast redwood, is the world's largest tree, towering high over a 30-storey skyscraper.

MIGHTY TREES

The trees we normally see around us, like apple trees, cherry trees, oaks, and maples, usually range from about 3 m (10 feet) to 25 m (80 feet) tall. At over 90 m (300 feet) tall, you can see how enormous the redwood is in comparison. These trees can grow in most parts of the world, but they only reach really incredible heights in one place – part of the coast of California.

AWESOMENESS

These monster trees tower above the rest.

SECOND BEST Another awesome tree, the giant sequoia, is the biggest living thing on the planet. It doesn't grow as tall as the redwood, but it is heavier. The biggest giant sequoia weighs more than 10 of the biggest blue whales.

A tornado spirals out from the clouds toward the ground.

TORNADO

A towering, roaring, twisting tornado is one of the most terrifying sights you could ever see. It's the most intense type of windstorm in the world. If a tornado lands on you, it can smash your home to matchwood in seconds, or even suck you up into the sky and fling you through the air.

TWISTING AND TURNING

Tornadoes form when hot and cold air meet, usually during a thunderstorm, and begin to twist and spiral around each other. The storm forms a whirling funnel shape reaching from the clouds toward the ground. It sucks dust and larger objects into it, and can move forward or suddenly 'hop'. The biggest tornadoes can be up to 4 km (2.5 miles) across.

KILLER TWISTERS

Tornadoes can happen in many places, but the most dangerous are in a part of the central United States known as 'Tornado Alley'. Every year a series of tornadoes destroys hundreds of houses and kills dozens of people.

DID YOU KNOW?

The fastest winds are found inside tornadoes. They can reach speeds of up to 500 km/h (300 mph).

AWESOMENESS

Tornadoes will blow you away!

Hurricane Jimena rips up Mexico.

AWESOMENESS

😀 😀 😀 😀 😀

Hurricanes (also called cyclones or typhoons) are the world's most awesome storms.

A satellite image of Hurricane Katrina raging over the southern coast of the United States.

HURRICANE

Tornadoes may have the fastest winds, but hurricanes are the biggest and most powerful storms of all. Like tornadoes, they are swirling spirals of wind — but they can be up to 1,500 km (930 miles) wide, bigger than many countries.

OCEAN MONSTERS

Hurricanes form over the surface of the sea in warm, tropical areas. The heat makes a lot of water evaporate into the air, and it forms clouds that whirl into a giant spiral. Hurricanes move across the ocean and often strike land, bringing awesome winds, huge waves, and torrential rain. This combination can be disastrous. Hurricanes such as Hurricane Katrina, which struck the city of New Orleans in 2005, and Hurricane Mitch, which hit Central America in 1998, can kill thousands of people with deadly floods and house-flattening winds.

THE EYE OF THE HURRICANE

Hurricanes really do have an 'eye' — a calm, quiet spot that's right in the middle of the storm. The clouds and winds circle around it, but in the centre, it's fairly still. If you're ever caught in a hurricane, don't think it's all over — it could be just the eye passing by!

EARTHQUAKE

As you go about your daily life you expect the ground to stay still. But there's no guarantee! The Earth's crust, which we all walk around on and build our houses on, is actually not fixed in place at all, and it can suddenly shake, shudder, ripple, or crack apart. Awesomely scary!

QUAKE ZONES

Earth's crust is made up of massive sections, or plates, floating around on molten rock, or magma. They're always slowly pushing and squeezing against one another. Sometimes, they get stuck. They push and push, building up pressure, until they suddenly slip. That's what causes an earthquake. Because of this, quakes are much more common in places that lie near the plate edges, or plate boundaries. These places include Japan, China, Indonesia, Italy, Greece, Chile, and the state of California.

QUAKE PANIC!

A big earthquake can cause havoc. Buildings and bridges fall down, water and gas pipes break, roads crack apart, and electricity wires snap. It's incredibly dangerous – earthquakes often kill thousands and thousands of people.

Major destruction is caused by an earthquake in Kobe, Japan, in 1995.

AWESOMENESS

😃😃😃😃

Earth's power is mind-blowing!

TSUNAMI

What's the biggest wave you've ever seen? Some seaside waves can be 12 m (40 feet) high – higher than a house. Storm waves at sea can reach 30 m (100 feet). But they get MUCH bigger than that. What about a 524-m (1,720 foot) high wave, as tall as a skyscraper, towering towards you? Tsunami waves can be this big – and tsunamis have many other striking qualities, too.

A giant wave slams into a promenade in the Basque Country, Spain.

SPLOSH!

The giant 524-m (1,720 foot) wave described above formed in 1958 at Lituya Bay, Alaska, after a landslide. A huge pile of rocks and mud crashed into the sea, making the water rise up and roll down the bay. Most tsunamis happen when an earthquake or landslide moves land next to or under the sea. This makes the sea move, too, and the tsunami wave sets off.

WET AND WILD

Often, a tsunami starts as a big ripple spreading out from where it started. At first, the wave can be quite low – just a few metres high.

But it's unusually long from front to back, and moves unusually fast. You may not notice it on the sea, but when it hits land, it causes disaster. It makes a large amount of water tower up into a big breaker, and crash onto the shore. Big tsunamis can flood the land, flattening buildings and sweeping people away.

AWESOMENESS

😬😬😬😬😬

A giant wall of water is one of the most powerful things nature can throw at us.

KILLER WAVES

Big tsunamis, such as the Indian Ocean tsunami of 2004, can kill thousands of people. People can be swept out to sea, squashed by collapsing buildings, or hit by debris.

DID YOU KNOW?

If the sea suddenly gets sucked away from the shore, leaving the sand bare, it usually means a tsunami wave is coming. Run inland and head for a high hill or a tall, strong building.

A lightning storm strikes Arizona, making a spectacular display.

LIGHTNING

We think of electricity as a modern thing for powering our computers and TVs – but it's also been crashing down out of the sky since Earth began. A lightning bolt is a giant electric spark, carrying a vast amount of energy. It is awesome to watch.

ELECTRIC CLOUDS

Lightning happens when a static electric charge builds up inside storm clouds. Movements inside them make electrons, tiny electric particles, collect at the bottom of a cloud. This eventually makes a spark jump across the gap between the ground and the cloud. The same kind of thing happens when you get a shock from a supermarket trolley – electric charge builds up, then a spark jumps into your body.

AWESOMENESS

😵😵😵😵

Crashingly loud, bright, and deadly, lightning is one of nature's most awesome shows.

STRUCK BY LIGHTNING

Lightning connects with high points on the ground and things that conduct, or carry, electricity. The electric shock and the heat from the lightning can be deadly.

Ball lightning makes a cool, but spooky sight in the sky.

BALL LIGHTNING

So you think you know what lightning's like? Well, ball lightning is a bit different. There's no flashing – just an eerie, glowing, floating ball of electrical energy. You've probably never seen it, as it's incredibly rare.

BALLS OF FIRE

In 1638, witnesses saw a glowing ball more than 2 m (6.5 feet) wide in a church in England during a thunderstorm. It smashed windows and walls, killing four people. In 1753, Georg Richmann also died when hit by a glowing ball while trying to do experiments in a thunderstorm. Similar balls have been seen in an Indian temple, in houses, inside airplanes and submarines – and there are thousands of other similar stories.

AWESOMENESS

It's not as powerful as normal lightning, but it's stranger and spookier, and awesomely bizarre.

WHAT CAUSES IT?

We don't know! Size seems to vary a lot. It can be deadly, but at other times it floats away. It seems to be associated with thunderstorms, and is probably electrical.

AURORA BOREALIS

If you're ever in the Arctic, or the north of Scandinavia, Russia, Canada, or Alaska, you may see an awesome, flickering, multi-coloured glow lighting up the night sky. This glow is the aurora borealis, or northern lights, and though the glow looks like fireworks or a laser show, it's completely natural.

The aurora borealis illuminates the sky over a tent in North America.

AWESOMENESS

This is a magical sight that you will never forget!

BITS OF THE SUN

The aurora borealis happens because the Sun throws out tiny particles in a stream known as the 'solar wind'. The particles are drawn toward the North and South poles by the Earth's magnetic field. When they crash into molecules in Earth's atmosphere, they make them give out light, creating an awesome effect.

WHEN CAN I SEE IT?

The solar wind varies, and the aurora is much stronger on some nights than others. It's also more common in spring and autumn. The further north you go, the better chance you have of seeing a good aurora if it's the right time of year, and the sky is dark enough.

MIRAGE

In cartoons and movies, people lost in the desert think they can see an oasis with palm trees and shimmering water . . . only to crawl up to it and find it's not there! This is called a mirage. It sounds unbelievable, but it really does happen and can be very convincing.

MAGIC MIRAGE

It seems impossible that you could see something in front of you that isn't there. But mirages can be explained. In a hot desert, the Sun heats up the ground, and the air just above the ground warms up, too. It's hotter than the air higher up. This makes separate layers of air. When light rays pass through the layers, the rays refract, or change direction, as they move from one layer to another.

A layer of hot air has created a mirror image of islands in the sky above the real islands.

FALSE IMAGE

This means that light rays coming from a faraway oasis or lake can bend on their way to your eyes. Your eyes see the object, but your brain thinks the light must have come in a straight line, so the image looks much closer. Sometimes, what looks like a lake is actually a mirage of a bit of the blue sky. Because of the light rays' bending, it appears to be lying on the ground ahead of you.

COOL EFFECTS

Mirages can make hot roads look as if they have puddles on them – but they disappear when you get closer. At sea, another type of mirage can make sailors see a ship that's actually very far away. Sometimes mirage ships appear to be sailing through the sky!

AWESOMENESS

Mirages are quite common, but rarely realistic enough to really fool you.

SAME SIZE? The Moon is 400 times smaller than the Sun, but because the Moon is closer to us, they look the same size; and in an eclipse, the Moon fits over the Sun.

An eclipse at 'diamond ring' stage, just before complete darkness.

DIAMOND RING In some eclipses, there is a moment when the whole Sun is covered except for a bright flash on one side, creating the 'diamond ring' effect.

SOLAR ECLIPSE

Long ago, when a solar eclipse turned the sky dark during the day, people were terrified. When it happens now, we all rush out to watch, wearing special protective glasses!

WHAT IS IT?

A solar eclipse, or eclipse of the Sun, happens when the Moon passes directly between the Sun and Earth. In a total eclipse, if you're standing in the right place, the Moon seems to cover the Sun completely, and casts a dark shadow on our planet. This happens only about once every 18 months. But partial eclipses, during which the Moon covers only part of the Sun, are more common and there are several every year.

WATCH WITH CARE

A solar eclipse is an amazing sight – but mind your eyes! As you know, staring at the Sun can damage your eyes. During an eclipse, you can buy special glasses that protect them so you can watch it happening.

AWESOMENESS

A solar eclipse is one of the most awesome and exciting of all natural events, and is both weird and thrilling to witness.

When first seen in 1604, Kepler's Star was the brightest star in the sky.

SUPERNOVA

A supernova happens when a large star runs out of fuel and nears the end of its life span. Some stars just cool or collapse when this happens, but a few get denser or heavier until they suddenly erupt.

SHINING STARS

To us on Earth, a supernova can look like a very bright, new star. This is because the explosion makes a faraway star we couldn't see before suddenly shine much more brightly. Then, after a year or so, it disappears again.

BLASTED TO BITS

As a supernova explosion happens, it blasts star matter out in all directions. Sometimes, this leaves behind a big space cloud of dust and gas, known as a nebula. New stars can form in a nebula when the dust starts to clump together again.

AWESOMENESS

It would be awesome up close, but on Earth, our experience of supernovae is a little calmer!

KEPLER'S STAR One of the most famous supernovae appeared in 1604, and disappeared a year later. It's named Kepler's Star after Johannes Kepler, a German astronomer who studied it. It was the last definite supernova sighting in our galaxy, but we now often see them in other galaxies.

A computer illustration of a pulsar, a rotating neutron star.

NEUTRON STAR

Sometimes, after an old, big star dies in a massive supernova explosion (see page 57), a neutron star is left behind.

MINI MONSTER

Think of how big the Sun is. A fairly typical, medium-sized star, the Sun is about 1.4 million km (870,000 miles) across – more than 100 times wider than Earth. In comparison, a neutron star is a tiny 20 km (12 miles) or so across. Yet a neutron star packs a punch – despite being so small, it's much heavier than the Sun. It's incredibly dense because it has collapsed and contains a huge amount of matter in a tiny space.

PULSARS

As a neutron star forms after a supernova explosion, it spins. As it collapses and gets smaller and denser, it rotates faster and faster. The spinning gradually slows down, but at the start of their lives, some neutron stars rotate many times per second. They give out beams of radiation that seem to us on Earth to flash or 'pulse' on and off as the star spins. Because of this, they are called pulsars.

SPOOKY STUFF When the first pulsar was discovered in 1967, some astronomers thought its regular pattern of flashes of energy could be a message from aliens trying to contact us.

BLACK HOLE

Black holes are among space's most mysterious objects. We can't see them because, as their name suggests, they're dark and stuff disappears into them. Unlike a star or planet, they don't shine in the night sky. But there are plenty of clues that they are there.

SPACE HOOVER

Scientists think black holes form after some types of stars die and completely collapse in on themselves. Their gravity pulls all their matter in so forcefully, they shrink to a tiny point that has no volume at all – it's just a dot. That's right – it's so small, it actually takes up no space at all! Yet it's massively heavy and has very powerful gravity. This sucks in the matter around it and even sucks in light. Scientists can spot black holes by the way the things around them swirl towards them and get sucked in.

WILL A BLACK HOLE GET US?

Black holes sound scary, but like any object with gravity, they only pull on matter that is close enough to them to be affected – just as our planet only pulls things to the ground once they're within its reach. A black hole won't grow and grow until it suddenly sucks in everything there is. So we can live with them in our Universe without a problem.

An artist's impression of a black hole with surrounding matter spiralling into it.

AWESOMENESS

Probably the most mind-melting concept you could try to work out.

SATURN'S RINGS

Saturn is 95 times the mass of our planet. This picture was taken by the Cassini spacecraft in 1997.

In 1610, the scientist and astronomer Galileo had a look at the planet Saturn with a telescope and was amazed to find that it had 'arms'. He thought they must have been moons. But when he looked again some time later, the arms had gone. What was going on?

MANY MOONS Besides its rings, Saturn also has an impressive collection of at least 62 moons.

WHAT ARE THE RINGS?
What Galileo had seen were Saturn's rings, which float around the planet. The main ring system is very wide, reaching out about 270,000 km (170,000 miles) beyond the planet, but also flat.

The rings look like a giant disc but are made up of separate bands. The bands are not solid but are made of chunks of rock and ice.

WHERE DID THEY GO?
When Galileo thought the rings had disappeared, it was because Saturn's position had changed, and he was seeing the rings from the side. Since they're so narrow, when this happens they become almost invisible.

MORE AWESOME STUFF Astronomers thought Saturn was the only ringed planet. But in the 20th century, scientists discovered that other planets of the outer solar system, Jupiter, Uranus, and Neptune, also have rings. They are fainter, dustier, and harder to see than Saturn's.

JUPITER'S GREAT RED SPOT

Jupiter is the biggest planet in our solar system, and you can identify it by the stripy yellow, beige, orange, and white bands that wrap around it. In many pictures of Jupiter you can also see a huge, swirling spot, a bit like an enormous eye.

SPECTACULAR SPOT

The Great Red Spot is actually a vast, extremely long-lasting storm. Jupiter is covered in clouds of water and other chemicals, which make up the stripes and bands swirling around it. Sometimes, they form into a spiral or cyclone, and the Great Red Spot is the biggest of these. It's so big that the whole of Earth could fit right inside it.

NEVER-ENDING STORM

On Earth, we're used to storms lasting a few days at the most. But the Great Red Spot has been swirling for at least 350 years!

DISAPPEARING SPOT

Astronomers have found that the spot is gradually shrinking. It used to be longer, but it's becoming rounder in shape and takes up less space.

AWESOME HUMAN CREATIONS

Look around you, and you'll see that we humans just can't stop building, creating, and inventing things. In this section you'll discover many of our most awesome creations. The world's tallest towers, widest bridges, most massive mines and dams, and most magical ancient monuments, temples, and ruins are all here — along with strange statues and skeleton-filled underground crypts. You'll also find the most mind-blowing machines, from the fastest cars and planes to the BIGGEST construction vehicles, the most high-tech robots, and even the world's fastest-zooming roller-coaster.

The Akashi bridge in Japan holds the record for the longest distance a bridge can stretch without touching the water or ground (see page 86).

GREAT PYRAMID OF GIZA

The ancient Greeks identified seven incredible places to visit, known as the Seven Wonders of the World. Only one of them, the Great Pyramid of Giza, is still standing for you to see today. It's the biggest of three huge pyramids built by the ancient Egyptians at Giza, near the city of Cairo, in Egypt.

PYRAMID POWER

The Egyptians built these pyramids as grand tombs for their leaders. Inside the Great Pyramid, long tunnels lead to chambers intended for Egyptian king Khufu's body and his treasure. But nothing remains of Khufu himself, and we don't know if he was ever actually buried there.

HOW DID THEY BUILD THEM?

To construct the Great Pyramid, more than 4,500 years ago, with no cranes, bulldozers, or power tools, the Egyptians managed to cut, shape, and haul more than two million blocks of stone, each weighing more than two cars, and fit them together into a perfect pyramid, 146 m (481 feet) high. Experts think they must have used teams of thousands of men, who pulled the blocks up earth ramps, perhaps on rollers made from logs.

AWESOMENESS

This giant, mysterious monument is one of the world's best-known tourist attractions.

THE SPHINX Near the three pyramids of Giza sits the Sphinx. This statue of a mythical beast with a lion's body and a human head is 73 m (240 feet) long and 20 m (66 feet) high.

CHICHÉN ITZÁ

Mexico, home of the ancient Mayan and Aztec peoples, has pyramids, too. The most awesome site of all is at the Mayan ruins of Chichén Itzá.

DID YOU KNOW?

As well as being temples, the Mayan pyramids were used for observing the night skies and charting the movements of the stars and planets.

RELIGIOUS RUINS

Chichén Itzá is a complex of several pyramids, buildings, carvings, and statues. It was an important centre of worship from about the year 900 to 1100.

EL CASTILLO

The biggest building at the site is known as El Castillo, meaning 'the Castle', but it's actually a pyramid with steps and a temple on top. It was built around 1,000 years ago and dedicated to Kukulcán, a feathered snake god. The staircases have carved snake heads at the top, and twice a year, the shadow of the steps at the corner of the pyramid moves down them in a slithery snake pattern.

GOING UP The staircases up each side of the pyramid make it easy to climb El Castillo, and tourists used to be able to walk up to the top. But after one person died by falling off the pyramid in 2006, this is no longer allowed.

EASTER ISLAND

WHAT A MESS!
Over the years, people raided Easter Island and most of the statues were pulled over, but now many of them have been restored.

In 1722, Dutch explorer Jacob Roggeveen was sailing in search of new lands in the southern hemisphere, when he stumbled across a tiny volcanic island in the Pacific Ocean. As it was Easter Day, he named the island Easter Island.

HUMONGOUS HEADS

The most remarkable thing about Easter Island is that it is dotted with enormous statues of humans up to 22 m (72 feet) tall, known as moai. These awesome statues are often called the 'Easter Island Heads'. They are whole body statues, but their heads are very large, and often the lower part of each statue was buried.

WHO LIVED HERE?

The moai were probably made by people who came from Polynesia, a group of Pacific islands. They worshipped their ancestors and this is probably who the statues represent. One statue can weigh up to 160 tonnes (145 tons), as much as 16 elephants, so it must have taken a huge effort to move the moai and stand them upright.

AWESOMENESS

Along with the mysteries of how and why they were made, the statues' faces add to their awesomeness.

The famous Easter Island heads are carved out of stone.

NAZCA LINES

On a high, flat stretch of the Peruvian Desert in South America, close to the town of Nazca, you can find hundreds of ancient lines and pictures cut into the ground. They're so vast that they only make sense when seen from the sky. How did they get there?

LONG-LASTING LINES

The Nazca Lines were made by lifting up the layer of red stones covering the surface of the desert to reveal the whiter rock underneath. Experts think the early Nazca people did this sometime between about 1,500 and 2,000 years ago. The patterns have survived to this day mainly because little rain or wind exists in the desert to move the stones or cover the lines again.

Some of the pictures are hundreds of metres across. This one is of a monkey.

PICTURE GALLERY

The patterns include very long, straight lines, spirals, triangles, other shapes, and animals. The lines can be several kilometres long. Experts think the Nazca people might have made them for their gods to look at, or to mark where water could be found.

A VIEW FROM THE SKY

Some people have suggested that the Nazca people must have been able to fly to be able to see the patterns. Others think the lines were laid out as runways for visiting alien spaceships!

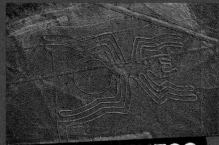

AWESOMENESS

The lines are magnificent, though you'll need a plane, balloon, or helicopter to see them at their best.

GOLDEN ROCK PAGODA

This awesome golden tower is 7 m (23 feet) tall, built on top of a big, gold-covered boulder that balances on top of another rock. It's in the country of Myanmar (also called Burma) in southeast Asia.

WOBBLE!

Amazingly, the rock the pagoda is built on is freestanding, and if you push it gently, it can wobble slightly on its perch.

WHAT IS A PAGODA?

There are many different types of pagodas, but they are usually tower-like buildings made up of several layers or tiers.

The Golden Rock Pagoda is a shrine for members of the Buddhist religion.

LEGEND According to legend, the pagoda was built when the Buddha, founder of the Buddhist religion, gave a hair from his head to a hermit. The hermit gave it to a king, telling him to keep it in a boulder shaped like the hermit's head. The king found the boulder, and built the pagoda to hold the hair.

CAPPADOCIA CAVE HOUSES

One of the Star Wars movies was partly filmed in Cappadocia, Turkey, because of its otherworldly, fantasy-like atmosphere. Tall towers of rock dot the landscape, and inside them are hundreds of cave houses, carved deep into the stone.

LIFE IN A CAVE

People have been living here for thousands of years. The rocks, formed by volcanic eruptions, then carved by wind and water into their shapes, are soft and easy to hollow out. People have given their caves windows, steps, and balconies.

EVERY CONVENIENCE

The houses keep cool all year round, and by digging deeper underground, people could make excellent hiding-places that protected them from attack.

WANT TO STAY? Several of the rock dwellings have been made into hotels, where you can go and stay to see what living in a cave house is like.

AWESOMENESS

😦 😦 😦

It's so awesomely strange here, it's like being in a fairy tale.

Some of the caves are now empty, but others are still people's homes.

COLOSSEUM

Rome, Italy's capital city, has lots of buildings dating from ancient Roman times, but the Colosseum has to be the most breathtaking of all. It's a massive amphitheater — an oval, open-air stadium where the Romans could watch their favourite sports and games.

GORY GAMES

The Roman entertainments were gory! Spectators went to see people called gladiators, who had to fight wild animals, or each other, to the death. Gladiators were usually slaves or criminals and were sent to the Colosseum as punishment. There wasn't much chance of survival, but those who did well and survived a lot of fights could win their freedom, and even become rich and famous.

ROMAN RUINS

The Colosseum was built out of stone from about 70 to 82 CE. Today, it's only partly still standing, as one section of it fell down during an earthquake in 1349.

AWESOMENESS

At 155 m (513 feet) across and almost 190 m (620 feet) long, this Roman building rivals many modern stadiums.

The Colosseum is an impressive building, even with part of it missing.

DID YOU KNOW?

The Romans used the Colosseum for several centuries. Tens of thousands of gladiators and wild animals probably died there.

TAJ MAHAL

The Taj Mahal, one of the world's most famous buildings, looks like an incredibly fancy white palace. But it was never meant to be lived in. In fact, it's a tomb – perhaps the most luxurious tomb on the planet.

AWESOMENESS

The Taj Mahal amazes thousands of visitors every day with its stunning beauty and romantic story.

MOURNING FOR MUMTAZ

The Taj Mahal stands near Agra, in India, and was built by an Indian emperor, Shah Jahan, for his wife Mumtaz Mahal. When she died in 1631, Shah Jahan was devastated and wanted to build the most beautiful monument he could in her memory. Mumtaz Mahal was buried there once the building was complete, and Shah Jahan joined her when he died in 1666.

LABOUR OF LOVE

The Taj Mahal, including its gardens and all its buildings, took just over 20 years to build. Around 20,000 building workers took part in the construction.

The beautiful Taj Mahal is made from white marble.

WHITE OVERNIGHT

Reports say that when Mumtaz died, Shah Jahan's grief was so great that his black hair turned white.

AWESOMENESS

😫 😫 😫 😫

Lost underwater cities normally belong to legends and fantasies – this one is real.

An artist's impression of Alexandria, the lost city beneath the sea.

ANCIENT ALEXANDRIA

Alexandria, on the coast of Egypt, was one of the greatest cities and was home to the Egyptian queen Cleopatra. It's now a modern city, but unlike other ancient cities, there are few ruins to be seen.

BENEATH THE WAVES

For many centuries, it was a well-known legend that much of Alexandria had disappeared into the sea. This was because of a series of earthquakes that shifted the land near the shore, making the city sink.

DISCOVERY

In the late 20th century, explorers began to dive in Alexandria's harbour in search of the lost city. Since 1996, archaeologist Franck Goddio and his team have discovered the ruins of the royal palace complex, streets, statues, and Alexandria's great library.

MIGHTY LIGHTHOUSE

Alexandria had an enormous lighthouse called the Pharos. Divers have discovered a base and stones, which are probably the Pharos' ruins.

MAHABALIPURAM

Near Mahabalipuram, in India, people have told stories about the sea swallowing up temples. These were considered myths, until divers came across building-like structures under the sea. . . .

HERE IT IS!

The 'myths' were so accurate that when explorers decided to search for the submerged ruins, around the year 2000, local fishermen took them to exactly the right spot and showed them where to start looking. They found what looked like the remains of streets and temples, stretching over an area of seabed so large it could have once been a big town.

POWER OF THE TSUNAMI

Mahabalipuram was hit by the huge Indian Ocean tsunami on December 26, 2004. The tsunami waves stirred up the seabed and washed away lots of the sand and silt that had collected around the ruins, revealing much more of them.

AWESOMENESS

There may be much more of this city yet to be found beneath the waves.

Shore Temple, one of the carved structures at Mahabalipuram.

YOU'RE JUST JEALOUS! One local legend says that the lost city at Mahabalipuram was so beautiful and perfect that the gods were jealous and sent the sea to drown it.

TERRACOTTA ARMY

Ancient Chinese emperor Shi Huangdi was only 13 when he began work on his tomb. The tomb had a pyramid, palaces, towers, and an army of at least 8,000 soldiers to guard him and help him rule his kingdom in the afterlife.

POTTERY WARRIORS

The soldiers buried weren't real people – they were made of terracotta, a kind of red clay. They are life-size or a bit bigger, and the emperor ordered that each one had to be an individual, with his own facial features. Archaeologists have found that they were made using moulds for different body parts and were then pieced together, before the final details of each face were added.

AWESOME FIND

The army lay buried near the city of Xi'an, in China, for more than two millennia, from the emperor's death in 207 BCE until 1974. Then, farmers digging a well came across some of the buried figures, and archaeologists gradually began to uncover the huge site.

AWESOMENESS

People come from all over the world to see these fascinating warriors on display.

The army includes soldiers of different ranks, as well as horses and chariots.

POMPEII

The awesome ruins at Pompeii, Italy, show us what a Roman town of 2,000 years ago looked like – just before it was flattened by an eruption from the nearby Vesuvius volcano.

MIGHTY ERUPTION

The eruption happened in 79 CE. The volcano had rumbled on for days before a pyroclastic flow took place. This is a flow of hot rocks, ash, and volcanic gas that erupts from some volcanoes (see page 37). People were either choked to death or were buried alive.

POMPEII TODAY

Pompeii remained buried for centuries, but in the 16th century it was rediscovered by an architect. Over the next few hundred years, several excavations uncovered more of the town.

WATCH OUT! Mount Vesuvius is still an active volcano, and today it looms over the major city of Naples, Italy. Three million people living close to it would be in danger if it erupts.

AWESOMENESS

Pompeii is a stunning record, both of Roman history and of a mind-blowing volcanic event.

Human remains were among the findings uncovered at the Pompeii site.

PARIS CATACOMBS

Catacombs are underground tunnels and chambers dug by humans. They can be hiding places, a place to hold religious ceremonies, or crypts for burying the dead. Under Paris, in France, lies a set of catacombs. It's an ossuary, where human skeletons are stored.

TOO MANY BONES!

In the past, Paris had a big problem with its overcrowded cemeteries. Bodies were buried together in big pits, then covered with dirt. After a while, when the flesh had rotted away, the skeletons were collected. But where did the bones go? In the late 1700s, officials decided some old, empty stone mines in the south of the city would make the perfect ossuary.

PICTURES AND PATTERNS

The bones were stacked up all around the walls of the catacombs' tunnels and rooms. They were sorted into different body parts and piled together, so they took up less space. People doing this job often used the bones to make patterns, shapes, and symbols.

AWESOMENESS

This underground world of bones is l something from a spooky video gam

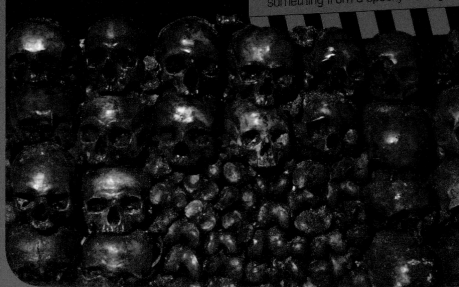

PALERMO CATACOMBS

The catacombs at Palermo, in Italy, are possibly even more creepy than those in Paris. Whole bodies stare down at you. And they're not just skeletons, either – they're mostly eerily preserved mummies, with much of their skin, flesh, and hair intact. Yikes!

MUMMIFIED MONK

It all started in 1599, when a monk was buried there. The local monastery had run out of burial space, so they decided to bury him in the vault under the church. They later discovered that the monk's body had not rotted away. When people heard about this unusual phenomenon, many wanted to be buried there. Burials carried on until 1920, and now there are thousands of mummies there.

WHAT MAKES A MUMMY?

Many of the mummies at Palermo have been treated to help preserve them. But the catacombs themselves are good at preserving bodies because the surrounding soil contains a rock called tufa that soaks up moisture. In a very dry atmosphere, things don't rot easily, and this helps keep the mummies fresh.

One of the mummified bodies in the catacombs at Palermo.

AWESOMENESS

In terms of spookiness, it doesn't get much more spine-chillingly creepy than this!

LOOK, DON'T TOUCH!

Tourists can visit the Palermo catacombs, but there are gates and railings in place to stop people from getting too close to the mummies. Before they were put in, people used to poke and prod the mummies, or pose next to them for photos!

USHIKU BUDDHA

The Ushiku Great Buddha, or Ushiku Daibutsu, is among the most famous Buddha statues, and is one of the biggest statues in the world. It stands in Ushiku, Japan, close to the capital, Tokyo.

WHAT IS A BUDDHA?

A Buddha is a holy figure in the Buddhist religion. The man who began this religion more than 2,400 years ago is known as the Buddha, but there are others. The Ushiku Buddha depicts a Buddha called Amitabha Buddha.

SNEAK A PEEK!

This isn't just a giant statue — it's also a museum! You can go inside to see Buddhist writings and many more (much smaller) statues. If you go up to the fourth level, you can also see out of the Buddha through narrow windows in his chest.

The Ushiku Buddha statue is an incredible 120 m (394 feet) tall.

AWESOMENESS

😀 😀

This giant statue looms breathtakingly over the landscape

PERFECTLY HAPPY

Buddha statues have expression of happiness on their faces. This is because they are said to have achieved perfect knowledge and contentment called nirvana.

MOUNT RUSHMORE

One side of Mount Rushmore in South Dakota is a surprising and awesome sight – four giant faces, carved into the grey granite cliffs, staring out over the landscape.

WHOSE FACES?

This amazing sculpture is a famous national monument. It shows the faces of four great presidents from history – George Washington, Thomas Jefferson, Theodore Roosevelt, and Abraham Lincoln. Each face is a gigantic 18 m (60 feet) high.

WHO MADE THEM?

A sculptor named Gutzon Borglum was asked to design and lead the project, and he began work in 1927 with a team of nearly 400 workers. It didn't always go smoothly – the first carving of Jefferson had to be blown up because the rock wasn't good enough to work with. Despite working on a high cliff using heavy equipment and explosives, no workers died during the construction, though a few were injured. The carving was finally declared complete in 1941.

The original plan was to show more of the presidents' bodies.

AWESOMENESS

There's no other sight quite like this in the world – nearly three million people go to see it each year.

GREAT WALL OF CHINA

The Great Wall of China is just that — a really huge, awesomely long wall that stretches across 7,200 km (4,470 miles) of northern China. Judging by the amount of material used to make it, it's the world's biggest human-made structure. If you walked along all of it, trekking for eight hours a day, it would take seven months.

BITS AND PIECES

However, you can't actually walk along the wall non-stop from one end to the other. It's not just one super-long structure, but is made up of many different sections, built at different times. The parts you often see in pictures are mostly near China's capital, Beijing, where the wall is especially large.

KEEP OUT!

People began building walls in this area 2,600 years ago. In 214 BCE, Emperor Shi Huangdi had more walls built and connected others to keep out invaders. Most of these walls have worn away. The wall as it is today was mostly built in the 1400s and 1500s to keep out Mongolian invaders.

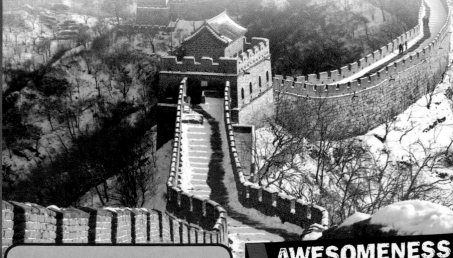

DID YOU KNOW? It really is an awesome wall, but don't believe anyone who tells you that astronauts can see it from space. This myth started before people even went into space!

AWESOMENESS

One of the world's most fascinating and famous structures.

PALM ISLANDS

For centuries, humans who needed more space have built into the sea, by filling it with rocks and sand to make land. The city of Dubai, in the Middle East, is building three awesome islands into the Persian Gulf, each shaped like a palm tree.

NOT ENOUGH BEACH!

Many people in Dubai wanted a house on the beachfront, but there was not enough beach for them all. This sparked the idea for the islands. Designers realized that palm-tree-shaped islands with lots of leaves would create many more kilometres of beach, where waterfront houses, hotels, and shops could be built. They planned three islands, each surrounded by a large ring of land to protect the island from heavy waves.

Palm Jumeirah, the first island – the other two islands will be even bigger.

GETTING STARTED

Work began on the first island, Palm Jumeirah, in 2001, and it's now mostly complete. It has most of its buildings and lots of people have moved into their homes. Two others, Palm Jebel Ali and Palm Deira, are under construction.

PARADISE? The first island has luxury homes and hotels, expensive stores and spas, and the weather is superhot. But it's not perfect – some residents have said that their houses are too close together, and that the sea between the branches is too still.

AWESOMENESS

It's awesome to see an island take shape from nothing – especially one that also forms a picture!

BURJ KHALIFA

The title of the world's tallest building rarely stays the same for long — new skyscrapers keep springing up and claiming the record. But in 2010, a new record-busting building was opened that should stave off its competitors for some time. The Burj Khalifa, in Dubai, is 828 m (2,717 feet) high — it towers over previous record-holders, beating them by more than 542 m (1,050 feet).

Excavation work for the Burj started in 2004. It is also the world's tallest freestanding structure.

WHAT'S IT FOR?

As well as being an awesome landmark and record-breaker, the Burj Khalifa has apartments, a luxury hotel, and offices inside it. Dubai's leaders also built it to make their city more famous and attract more tourists and publicity. It worked!

TRIANGULAR TOWER

The Burj (meaning 'tower') is an unusual shape, and looks like a space-age needle poking into the sky. Its cross-section is Y-shaped, with three sections sticking out around it, getting narrower towards the top. This makes it very strong, and also means lots of the rooms inside can have windows. The tower has an amazing 162 floors!

WOOHOO! LET'S JUMP OFF The tower first opened on 4th January, 2010, and just four days later, two **BASE** jumpers got the chance to break the world record for a parachute jump off a building by leaping from floor 160, 672 m (2,205 feet) from the ground. They both landed safely.

BINGHAM CANYON MINE

Bingham Canyon is still a busy working mine, but it also has a visitors' centre.

The Bingham Canyon Mine in Utah is the world's largest and most awesome hole! It's the biggest excavation ever made by humans. If you fly over it, you see it gaping below you among the mountains like a huge drain in the ground.

HOW DID IT GET THERE?

It's taken nearly 150 years for miners to hollow out such a massive mine. They began work in 1863 after discovering that the ground in this area contained valuable minerals. The mine grew and grew, and railways and towns sprang up around it. Today, it's still getting bigger and deeper, and more than 1,000 people work there.

MOUNTAINS OF METAL

Bingham Canyon is mainly a copper mine, and has produced over 16.3 million tonnes (18 million tons) of copper – as well as large amounts of more valuable silver and gold. Copper is in huge demand as it has all kinds of uses – from its use in household pipes and electric wires to coins, cooking pans, and computer circuits.

HOW MUCH STUFF? Altogether, more than 6 billion tonnes (6.6 billion tons) of material have been dug out of the mine to leave a hole nearly 4 km (2.5 miles) wide and more than 1.2 km (0.75 mile) deep. It's so deep that it could easily swallow up the world's tallest building, the Burj Khalifa.

LAKE PONTCHARTRAIN CAUSEWAY

Imagine zooming off the shore, away from land, onto a road surrounded by water. This is what it's like on the longest water-crossing bridge, the Lake Pontchartrain Causeway.

LONG AND LOW

The longest bridges of all are causeways — low, simple, road-like bridges that rest on supports standing on the sea or riverbed. Lake Pontchartrain Causeway stretches a massive 39 km (24 miles).

WHAT'S IT FOR?

Lake Pontchartrain is a salty lake connected to the sea, next to the city of New Orleans. The bridge goes right across the middle of it, connecting New Orleans to the city of Mandeville on the other side of the lake. It lets people whizz to work quickly instead of driving all around the lake.

This awesome bridge is so long that you can't see dry land when you're standing at the halfway point.

AWESOMENESS

It's not just mind-blowingly long, it's also weird and wonderful to ride across.

I WANT TO GO BACK!

The bridge is made up of two separate roads — one for each direction. So you can't just do a U-turn if you change your mind!

MILLAU VIADUCT

The Millau Viaduct in France is the world's highest bridge. It's pretty long, too, at nearly 2.4 km (1.5 miles), but what makes it so awesome is the way it towers above the landscape, and carries you out into the middle of empty space.

THE HIGH ROAD

The bridge was built on a tourist route in the south of France, where cars were getting clogged up and stuck every summer. They had to drive down into a deep valley, past the little town of Millau, and then drive all the way back up again. The bridge cuts out that stage, soaring right across the valley and the river Tarn.

FLYING HIGH

The bridge smashed more than one record when it was opened in 2004. It has the tallest towers of any bridge. They reach 343 m (1,125 feet) high, taller than the Eiffel Tower. It also has the world's highest road bridge, rising 270 m (886 feet) above the river Tarn. Looking down from it is like peering off a 100-storey skyscraper. The bridge is made of steel and weighs 36,000 tonnes (40,000 tons), as much as 250 blue whales.

The slight curve of the Millau Viaduct helps drivers get a thrilling view.

RUNNER UP The Petronas Towers in Malaysia, once the tallest building in the world, have another scarily high bridge. It's a footbridge that links the two Petronas Towers, and is 170 m (558 feet) up in the air.

AWESOMENESS

This incredible structure is truly breathtaking.

AKASHI-KAIKYO BRIDGE

Perhaps the most awesome bridge record is the biggest single span – the longest distance a bridge can stretch without touching the water or the ground at all. This award goes to Japan's Akashi-Kaikyo Bridge, across the sea between two of Japan's islands.

DID YOU KNOW? Before the bridge was built, you had to cross the Akashi Strait by ferry. But the sea there can be stormy and difficult for ferries to cross. The bridge makes the trip much safer for the thousands of cars that cross the strait every day.

SUSPENDED IN SPACE

Suspension bridges have the longest spans of any bridges. Most suspension bridges have two towers, with cables overhead. At each end, the cables are fixed in the ground. Between the towers, they support the bridge's main span.

AWESOME AKASHI

Akashi-Kaikyo has a central single span that measures 1,991 m (6,532 feet) long. It had to be made this way because the sea channel it crosses, the Akashi Strait, is very important for big ships. The bridge needed a wide, high central span to let them through easily. Building it took 10 years, and its cables contain enough steel wire to circle the planet seven times!

The Akashi-Kaikyo Bridge is 1.5 times longer than the Golden Gate Bridge.

THREE GORGES DAM

China's massive Three Gorges Dam on the Yangtze River is one of the world's most controversial building projects ever. But that's not its only claim to fame.

RECORD BUSTER

This dam is a monster – it has one of the world's biggest dam walls. Since it started running in 2009, it's the biggest electricity-generating power station on the planet. Its hydroelectric turbines produce enough power to run a big city.

GOOD OR BAD?

As well as generating electricity, the dam controls the flow of the River Yangtze, helping prevent the floods that have killed thousands. But the lake behind the dam flooded other land, forcing people to move, and drowning farmland, wildlife, and ancient ruins.

Floodwater is diverted and controlled by the Three Gorges Dam.

TROLL A GAS PLATFORM

Troll A, a rig for extracting useful natural gas from underneath the North Sea, is the biggest gas platform on the planet. When it was first completed, it was the tallest and heaviest object humans have ever moved from one place to another.

DADDY LONGLEGS

The rig now rests on the seabed on its four enormous concrete legs. They stand in water more than 369 m (1,210 feet) tall. Each leg is a vast, hollow tube of steel-reinforced concrete.

GETTING THE GAS

Being so big, strong, and sturdy allows Troll A to stand firmly in place as it drills into the seabed to pipe out natural gas, used for heating, cooking, and power stations. At any one time, there are up to 300 people working on the rig.

The Troll A Platform being towed into place before being lowered onto the seabed.

AWESOMENESS

😫 😫 😫 😫

This is one of the most awesome engineering feats ever.

GOING DOWN . . . The Troll A Gas Platform used air-filled tanks to help it float so it could be towed over 200 km (120 miles) into position, before being submerged.

CAPE HATTERAS LIGHTHOUSE

The Cape Hatteras Lighthouse, on Hatteras Island, North Carolina, is the tallest in the United States, and the biggest in the world made of brick. It stands over a part of the sea known as 'the graveyard of the Atlantic' due to its dangerous sandbars, storms, and currents.

AWESOMENESS

😵 😵

Although it's not the tallest of structures, Cape Hatteras is an impressive landmark.

Over the course of 23 days, the lighthouse was carefully moved 870 m (2,870 ft) from its original position (left) on huge steel beams (centre) to its new position away from the pounding waves (right).

A MILLION BRICKS

The lighthouse is made of more than 1,200,000 bricks and stands at 64 m (210 feet) tall. It has 248 steps, which you can use to go up to the top. In clear weather, the revolving light, which turns every seven seconds, can be seen up to 40 km (25 miles) away.

GOING ON A JOURNEY

This large lighthouse has been moved a long way from its original position. Since it was built in 1870, the sea has eroded the land and moved closer to the bottom of the tower. So in 1999, it was very slowly and carefully shifted inland. Many thought it would collapse, but it survived. Awesome!

STRIPY DAYMARK Cape Hatteras Lighthouse is painted in a unique black-and-white, diagonal-striped pattern. This is so that during the day, sailors can tell which lighthouse it is and work out where they are. A lighthouse's own pattern of stripes and colours is called its daymark.

AWESOMENESS

This crane is the most powerful lifting machine on the planet!

TAISUN CRANE

Most of the cranes that you see on building sites are tall, spindly things that are designed for lifting bundles of bricks or pipes high up onto buildings under construction. However, these cranes aren't very strong, and they're often not very stable either. When you need super-sturdy, awesome lifting power, you need the Taisun crane.

HOW BIG IS IT?

Taisun is made of two strong concrete towers, which are fixed to the ground, with two beams across the top of them. The crane is 114 m (374 feet) tall, dwarfing most of the world's cranes. It can be found in the Yantai Raffles shipyard in China.

MUSCLE MAN

At its opening ceremony in April 2008, Taisun lifted a barge to confirm its status as the strongest crane on the planet.

The Taisun crane towers over the shipyard as it carries out its heavy lifting work.

CRANE COLLAPSES Conventional tall, narrow cranes topple over or break quite often. One collapsed onto a building in New York in 2008, killing seven people. Later that year, another crane collapsed not far away, killing two construction workers.

BAGGER 293

Now this is awesome. You've seen diggers. Maybe you've seen BIG diggers. But there's no digger as big, brawny, and breathtaking as the brain-boggling Bagger 293.

BUCKETS ON A WHEEL

Instead of having one big scoop on the end of a digging arm, the Bagger is a bucket-wheel excavator. This means it has a digging wheel that is like a waterwheel, with 18 digging scoops around the edge. As the wheel turns, the 'buckets' grab scoopfuls of earth, then dump them on a conveyor belt so that they can be collected and carried away.

BIGGEST BAGGER

Bagger 293 is 225 m (738 feet) long and 96 m (315 feet) high. That's as long as 18 buses and higher than some high-rises. Even the bucket wheel on its own measures 21 m (70 feet) across—that's as high as a seven-story building. The Bagger weighs about 12,880 tonnes (14,200 tons), which is about a thousand times heavier than an average digger.

Bagger 293 is the biggest, but there are other similar Baggers.

The Bagger's mighty bucket wheel is huge!

KINGDA KA ROLLER COASTER

AWESOMENESS

People who've ridden Kingda Ka often say it feels so fast that they were sure it had gone wrong!

Do you like really fast, really high roller-coasters? Then you'll love Kingda Ka, at Six Flags Great Adventure park in New Jersey, USA. It holds the record for highest, fastest roller-coaster on the planet.

SHORT SHARP SHOCK

Kingda Ka catapults you along as fast as possible, then flings you up into the sky over the top of a giant 'top hat' – a roller-coaster term for a very tall hill with almost vertical sides.

WHAT'S IT LIKE?

At first, the coaster train chugs along to a launching area before accelerating up to 206 km/h (128 mph) in less than four seconds. The g-force slams your head back against the seat and flattens your face. Then, when you've reached top speed, you climb up over the top hat to a height of 139 m (456 feet), before zooming and twisting down again almost vertically. The train then sails over another, smaller hill, giving you a sense of zero gravity, before coming to a stop.

Passengers zoom down Kingda Ka after climbing and speeding down the top hat.

WHY 'KINGDA KA'? Lots of people have wondered if the name 'Kingda Ka' has some kind of meaning, but it seems it's just a made-up name. A tiger at the same theme park is also called Kingda Ka.

SPIRIT OF AUSTRALIA

You might expect the fastest boat ever to be a flashy new model stuffed to the brim with all the latest technology. In fact, the boat that holds the record, the *Spirit of Australia*, was built in the early 1970s and clocked its world record speed years ago, in 1978.

I MADE IT MYSELF!

The *Spirit of Australia* was actually designed and made by Australian speedboat enthusiast Ken Warby in his own garden, using fibreglass, wood, and a Westinghouse J34 jet engine, which is normally used on jet planes. Although it was homemade, the boat has a space-age design, and looks like a jet plane without wings.

SMASHING THE RECORD

After several years of trials, Warby broke the world water speed record on 20th November, 1977, driving the *Spirit of Australia* at 464 km/h (288 mph), which is as fast as some planes fly. The following year, he achieved an even faster speed of 511 km/h (317 mph), a record that stands to this day.

The *Spirit of Australia*, *the world's fastest boat, sits on display.*

AWESOMENESS

😠😠😠😠😠

This boat's record is awesome, especially since the boat is homemade.

Ken Warby in his record-breaking boat – the Spirit of Australia.

KNOCK NEVIS

Tankers are ships that carry oil around the world. Since we use oil to fuel cars, planes, and power stations, we need A LOT of it — so, over the years, tankers have become bigger. The biggest of all are called supertankers, and the biggest ever was the *Knock Nevis*.

GIANT OF THE SEA

The *Knock Nevis* is sadly no longer sailing. Like all ships it eventually wore out and became unseaworthy. But it remains the longest ship ever built, at just over 458 m (1,504 feet) long. To walk from one end of the ship to the other would take you about seven minutes. The massive deck had enough space for 25 Olympic-size swimming-pools.

WHAT'S IN A NAME?

The *Knock Nevis* has had many different names in its lifetime. Usually, the name changed when it changed hands and was used for different jobs. It began life in 1979 as the *Seawise Giant*, then became the *Happy Giant*, the *Jahre Viking*, and then the *Knock Nevis*. Finally, on the way to be scrapped, it was given its last name: *Mont*.

AWESOMENESS

😄😄😄😄

PARRRP! You couldn't miss this monster sailing past.

The mighty **Knock Nevis** *ploughs through the water.*

DID YOU KNOW? The *Knock Nevis* was so big and heavy that when fully loaded, it couldn't sail up the English Channel or through either of the giant Suez or Panama ship canals. It would have scraped along the bottom and become stuck.

OASIS CLASS CRUISER

How about setting foot on an enormous cruise ship like the Oasis class cruisers? These ships, the biggest passenger ships on Earth, look like floating giant luxury apartment buildings.

Wall-climbing is just one of the many activities on cruise ships likes these.

OASIS OF THE SEAS

There are two Oasis class cruisers – the first to be completed was the *Oasis of the Seas*, in 2009. It stands up to 72 m (236 feet) above the water and has 16 decks. It can carry more than 6,000 passengers, along with a crew of at least 2,000 to look after them and run the ship.

This humongous cruise ship contains just about everything you could want.

AWESOME ATTRACTIONS

Cruise ships take people on luxury long-distance journeys – they stop at exotic locations and have entertainment on board. The *Oasis of the Seas* has theatres, nightclubs, swimming-pools, gyms, theme parks, a golf course, climbing walls, ice rinks, and even a park filled with trees and tropical plants and surrounded by shops.

DID YOU KNOW?

A cruise ship this big needs its own hospital, water treatment plant, and security team.

BLACKBIRD

This futuristic machine looks like something from a sci-fi movie. In fact, it's a real plane, the Lockheed SR-71 Blackbird, and it's one of the world's most famous fighter planes. It holds the record for the fastest manned, air-breathing aircraft.

NNNEEEEOOOWWW!

Just how fast can it go? Faster than a speeding bullet, and faster than Earth's rotation, so in a Blackbird, you can travel around the world from east to west and stay ahead of the Sun in the sky. In July 1976, one Blackbird (32 were made altogether) set a speed record of 3,529 km/h (2,193 mph), which has never been beaten by another plane in its class. An 'air-breathing' aircraft is one with an engine that takes in air, unlike a rocket-powered plane, which can go faster.

SPY PLANE

The Blackbird was used by the United States to spy on enemies and zoom away. Its dark colour and streamlined shape helped it to avoid being spotted by radar systems. It flew on missions from 1964 until 1995, when it was retired – although some of the planes are still used for tests, and you can see others at museums.

AWESOMENESS

😖😖😖😖😖

Of all the planes in the world, this is the most mind-blowing, as well as being a speed record-holder.

DID YOU KNOW?

The SR-71 is known as the Blackbird, but it was never officially named that – it's just a nickname.

The Blackbird's dark colour was chosen to blend in with the night sky.

ANTONOV AN-225

This fabulous flying machine isn't especially fast — it's just vast! The Russian-built Antonov An-225 *Mriya* is the biggest fixed-wing aircraft in the world.

The Antonov makes an impressive sight in the sky.

SPECIAL DELIVERY!

This awesome aircraft could hold hundreds of people, but it's mainly used as a cargo plane. It was designed to transport the *Buran*, a space shuttle developed in Russia in the 1980s, but this space programme was cancelled. Instead, it can now be hired out for carrying any mighty object you like — sections of spacecraft or aircraft, trains, or massive construction machines. It is also used to deliver emergency supplies to disaster areas.

VITAL STATISTICS

So how big is it? The Antonov measures 84 m (276 feet) long and has a wingspan of 88 m (290 feet). It has six powerful jet engines and 32 landing wheels. Items that are too big to fit inside the cargo hold can be fixed to the roof — this is how the *Buran* space shuttle was transported.

The Antonov transports the Buran *space shuttle to Kiev, in the Ukraine.*

DID YOU KNOW? With most famous planes, such as the Blackbird and Concorde, a fleet of planes were built — but there's only one Antonov An-225. Its name, *Mriya*, means 'dream'. Another matching plane was planned, but it was never finished.

A Lynx helicopter lets off flares as it hovers over a Dutch navy ship.

A Lynx helicopter in the Arctic.

LYNX

If you were stuck in a war zone, injured or lost behind enemy lines, you'd be over the Moon to see a Lynx coming to get you. It's the world's fastest helicopter, as well as one of the most reliable. This classic helicopter has been flying since 1971 and is still used all over the world, mostly by the armed forces.

MULTITASKER

Besides its awesome speed, the Lynx can climb fast vertically, hover safely, and land in a small area. It can hold nine people (as well as its two crew members), carry cargo, or swoop through the sky on spying missions. It's great at search and rescue operations, and it can also be a fighter, carrying antisubmarine or anti-tank missiles.

THE RECORD

A Lynx holds the record for the fastest helicopter flight. The record was set in 1986 by pilot John Trevor Egginton. His modified demonstration model flew at just over 400 km/h (249 mph). It's probably not possible for a normal helicopter to go much faster than this – the forces on the rotor blades could rip them apart.

AWESOMENESS

It is a normal-looking helicopter, but is a force to be reckoned with.

DID YOU KNOW?

The Lynx is so popular that countries all over the world have ordered it from Britain.

AWESOMENESS
😵 😵 😵 😵
Wow – this car doesn't just go
awesomely fast; it looks
awesomely cool, too.

ThrustSSC's massive engines provide it with incredible power.

THRUSTSSC

Imagine if this was what was sitting in your garage! It hardly looks like a car at all – and it's not something you'd cruise to the supermarket in – but it is a car, and it's the fastest on the planet. It's called the ThrustSSC – SSC stands for 'supersonic car'.

BREAKING THE SOUND BARRIER

As its name suggests, ThrustSSC can reach supersonic speeds, speeds that are faster than the speed of sound. It set the world land speed record in 1997, driven by a British Royal Air Force pilot, Andy Green. Zooming across a flat desert in Nevada, he reached a speed of 1,228 km/h (763 mph). The speed of sound is around 1,225 km/h (761 mph).

HOW?

ThrustSSC was designed and built by British pilot and aircraft engineer Richard Noble and his team. It's powered by two mighty jet engines – Rolls Royce Spey turbojet engines, which are usually used on aircraft. The car's streamlined, ground-hugging shape helps it to whizz through the air while staying firmly on course.

COMPETITION FOR THE THRUSTSSC Richard

Noble is now working on a new supersonic car, the BloodhoundSSC, and hopes it will smash ThrustSSC's land speed record. Keep an eye out for it!

AIRBUS A380

As more and more people want to fly around the world, passenger airliners get bigger and bigger. Since 2007, the world's biggest passenger aircraft has been the Airbus A380, also known as the 'Superjumbo'.

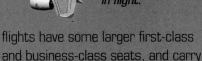

The Airbus A380 in flight.

BUS OF THE SKIES

If you've ever seen or flown on a Boeing 747, you'll immediately see the difference with this plane. A 747 is big, but has an upper deck only at the front. The A380 has upper and lower decks all the way through, like a double-decker bus. It can carry more than 800 passengers, if all the seats are economy-sized – though most flights have some larger first-class and business-class seats, and carry 500–600 people.

LIFE OF LUXURY

Since the A380 has more room than other passenger jets, airlines have tried to come up with ways to make the space more fun and glamorous. In their most expensive and luxurious sections, some A380s have double bedrooms, showers, a private first-class bar, or a gym!

The A380 has been designed to be quieter than other big airliners, which is good news if you live near an airport.

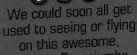

AWESOMENESS

We could soon all get used to seeing or flying on this awesome, spacious Superjumbo.

ROCKET PLANE

What is a rocket plane? It's just what it sounds like – a rocket-powered plane that's a cross between an airplane and a spaceship. It can fly far higher than a normal plane and take pilots or passengers to the edge of space. Then it can descend and land on a runway like any other plane.

SPEEDING TO SPACE

A rocket engine is an engine that burns fuel and forces out gases at incredible speed. For much of the 20th century, inventors were developing rockets to use for space travel, and rocket planes developed alongside them.

The fastest ever was the North American X-15, which now holds the record for the fastest manned aircraft. In 1967, an X-15 flown by US pilot Pete Knight achieved the record speed of 7,274 km/h (4,520 mph).

SPACE TOURISTS

Some rocket planes take tourists to experience space. This costs a lot, but not as much as going into orbit in a space rocket. The most famous passenger rocket plane is probably SpaceShipTwo, owned by the Virgin business group. It's designed to fly at speeds of more than 4,000 km/h (2,485 mph) and soar to at least 110 km (63 miles) above Earth's surface, while carrying up to six passengers.

X-15 DISASTER

Although space tourism flights will be made as safe as possible, flying to space can be risky. One X-15 pilot, Michael James Adams, died in 1967 after his rocket plane began to spin and shake, before falling apart in the air.

VOYAGER 1

Far away, out in the darkness of space, *Voyager 1* is on a long, bold, lonely journey. This little space probe has travelled further away from our planet than any other human-made object. It was sent to explore the Solar System and take messages about Earth to whoever might one day find it.

This gold-plated aluminum cover protects the Golden Record.

AWESOMENESS

Voyager 1's journey is awesome, and it's even more amazing to think about where it could end up.

SOLAR SYSTEM MISSION

Voyager 1 was launched in 1977. To begin with, its job was to explore the planets with its onboard cameras and measuring equipment, and send data back to Earth using radio signals. It took stunning pictures of Saturn and Jupiter and some of their moons. Now it has left the Solar System, and is moving through interstellar space.

ATTENTION, ALIENS!

Both *Voyager 1* and its sister probe, *Voyager 2* (which has not travelled quite as far), carry a 'Golden Record'. These records contain information about Earth that could one day be discovered by intelligent life elsewhere in the Universe. They include recordings of animal noises, human languages, and music, pictures of Earth and humans, and scientific data.

An artist's impression of the Voyager spacecraft.

DO ALIENS EXIST?

No one knows for sure. But other stars have planets around them, and space is so huge that many think it's likely that other life-forms exist.

HUBBLE SPACE TELESCOPE

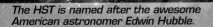
The HST is named after the awesome American astronomer Edwin Hubble.

Wouldn't it be awesome to have a time machine that could look back billions of years? Well, we already have something like that – the **Hubble Space Telescope (HST)**. The HST is a superpowerful telescope that flies in orbit around Earth. It was launched in 1990 and is still working today.

The HST during the Space Shuttle Endeavour's mission to service it.

TIME TRAVEL? HOW?

We use the Hubble for looking at the furthest away known parts of space. Remember that light takes time to zoom across space. Although light goes incredibly fast, distant galaxies are so far away that the light from them takes ages to get here. A light-year is the distance light travels in a year. If an object is 10 billion light-years away, that means light from it has taken 10 billion years to reach us. And THAT means that when we see it, we are seeing how it looked 10 billion years ago!

HOW HUBBLE WORKS

The HST collects light from stars, galaxies, planets, and other space sights through the end of a tube. Inside the tube is a very polished, curved mirror that reflects the light and focuses it to a clear image. This is then recorded by cameras and other sensors.

HELIOS SPACECRAFT

AWESOMENESS

😬 😬 😬 😬

This is the fastest thing humans have ever made – well done, us!

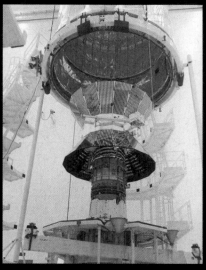

A prototype of the Helios spacecraft in 1974.

There are some awesomely fast machines in this book – but compared with the Helios space probes, most of them look like half-asleep snails. Two of these high-tech probes, *Helios 1* and *Helios 2*, were sent to orbit the Sun in the 1970s. They were both superspeedy, but *Helios 2* was slightly faster. It holds the record for fastest human-made object ever.

THE FASTEST MACHINE

As *Helios 2* whizzed close to the Sun, it reached a maximum speed of 252,792 km/h (157,078 mph). That's 4,213 km (2,618 miles) every minute, or 70 km (43 miles), every second. If you could fly that fast, you could zoom right around the world, back to where you started, in nine and a half minutes. Or you could go from home to school in the time it takes to blink!

OVAL ORBITS

The Helios probes reached such speed because they were sent into elliptical, or oval, orbits around the Sun. Scientists wanted them to study the Sun from different distances, and an elliptical orbit allowed this. When an object is in an elliptical orbit around something, it flies more slowly when it is furthest away, then, pulled by gravity, speeds up massively as it comes closer. The Sun's superpowerful gravity catapulted the probes past it at enormous speeds.

DID YOU KNOW? The Helios probes stopped working about 10 years after they launched, so they no longer send us data. But they're still there, whizzing around the Sun roughly once every 190 days.

INTERNATIONAL SPACE STATION

Floating in orbit above the Earth's surface is an awesome place where you can actually go and live. It's the International Space Station (ISS), a permanent space base where astronauts study Earth and space science, and try to find out more about what life in space does to our bodies.

Astronauts on a spacewalk, working on the International Space Station.

The International Space Station on its orbit around the Earth.

BUILDING PROJECT

As well as performing their scientific work, the astronauts who go to the ISS build more parts on it. Building began in 1998, and astronauts have been living there since 2000. Today, the station includes living quarters, science labs, and storage and service decks. It also has docking bays and an air lock so that visiting spacecraft can link to it, and astronauts can spacewalk outside.

A DAY IN SPACE

The astronauts have to live with very low gravity where things float around. Food and drinks are eaten from closed bags. The toilets have powerful suction to pull everything away. The crew sleep in sleeping bags that are tied to the walls.

AWESOMENESS

This awesome structure turns sci-fi stories of life in space into a reality.

SHANGHAI MAGLEV

If you're ever in Shanghai, China, you can go for a 'flight' on one of the world's fastest, most high-tech trains. It's called a flight because this train service uses maglev (magnetic levitation) technology, which means the trains don't actually touch the ground as they zoom along!

AIRPORT SHUTTLE

This superfast train doesn't actually have a very long journey to make. It links the suburbs of the busy capital of Shanghai to its airport, and only covers a distance of 30 km (19 miles). Its top speed on the journey is around 430 km/h (267 mph), though in test runs, the train has topped 501 km/h (311 mph).

FLOATING ON AIR

Maglev trains are awesome. They use powerful electromagnets to make the train levitate or hover just above the track. A system of magnetic forces can also be used to pull the train forwards, and make it brake. It's easier for maglev trains to reach superhigh speeds, as there's no friction between the train and the track.

RUNNER-UP The Shanghai Maglev isn't the fastest train ever – that record is held by Japan's JR-Maglev train, which reached 581 km/h (361 mph) in 2003. But this speed was made on a special test run, using a modified train that you can't ride on. So the Shanghai Maglev is the fastest working passenger train.

The Shanghai Maglev train zooms away from the city's airport.

AWESOMENESS

😆 😆 😆

Whizzing along on this train really does feel like flying.

TRANS-SIBERIAN RAILWAY

On the Trans-Siberian Railway, you won't be zooming at hundreds of kilometres per hour, or anywhere even close. But you can experience an awesomely long train trip, as this is the world's longest railway.

WHERE IS IT?

The Trans-Siberian Railway stretches right across Russia from Moscow, the capital, which is close to European countries such as Estonia and Finland, to Vladivostok, on Russia's east coast near Japan. It gets its name because it crosses the area of northern Russia called Siberia, but in fact, it also winds its way across most of the width of Asia. The railway is 9,198 km (5,778 miles) long, and is one of the world's longest continuous rail journeys.

TAKE A TRIP!

You could make this journey much faster by plane, but lots of tourists travel on the Trans-Siberian to experience its famous route. It takes about a week and crosses seven time zones! The trains have sleeper cabins or sofas that convert into beds. At many stations, the train waits to allow people to get off and buy food.

AWESOMENESS

😆 😆 😆 😆

If you love trains, you'll want to travel on the Trans-Siberian Railway. It's an awesome adventure!

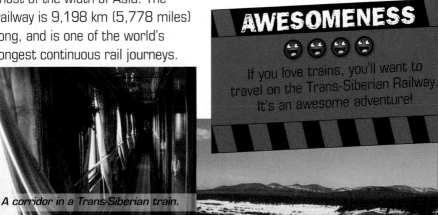

A corridor in a Trans-Siberian train.

A train travelling to Vladivostok on the Trans-Siberian Railway.

LARGE HADRON COLLIDER

Despite our high-tech inventions, there are questions we haven't answered. One of them is the nature of matter – the stuff that everything is made of. Your books, computer, even your hands – we know they're made of atoms and molecules – but what are THEY made of? How does matter work? How did it start to exist?

LET'S FIND OUT

Since the 1900s, scientists have been trying to look at matter, and in about 1930, they came up with the particle accelerator. It's a machine that smashes tiny bits of matter together at high speeds, making them break and change, so we can study them. We now have a new particle accelerator, the Large Hadron Collider (LHC).

ROUND IN A RING

The LHC is made up of a huge, 9-km-wide (6 mile), hollow ring, buried deep under the ground near Geneva, Switzerland. It uses a series of electromagnets to control beams of particles, making them fly around the ring. The LHC officially began operating in 2008, but it sometimes has to be switched off for repairs.

The magnet core of the LHC.

AWESOMENESS

😵 😵 😵 😵 😵

This machine is awesome to look at and has a truly important job to do.

We use trace patterns like these to study how particles behave.

THE END OF THE WORLD? When the LHC was about to be switched on, some people feared it could destroy the planet by creating a black hole (see page 59). Scientists, however, don't think this is likely.

MAUNA KEA OBSERVATORY

How would you like to go to work on top of a volcano, on an island in the middle of the Pacific? If you become an astronomer, maybe you can. On top of Mauna Kea, a dormant volcano in Hawaii, stands the world's most awesome observatory, or space-viewing station.

WHY HERE?

Mauna Kea's summit is 4,205 m (13,796 feet) tall, and is the highest point of Hawaii's Big Island. Though that's not as high as giants like Mount Everest, it's still a massive mountain and its summit is higher than most of the clouds that form around it. Far from big cities, the air is clean and the skies are very dark. And it's near the equator, giving a good view of the whole sky. It's probably the best place on earth's surface to put a telescope.

TELESCOPES GALORE

All over and around the summit stand 13 different, awesomely high-tech telescopes, owned and run by various countries and organizations from around the world. Most powerful of all is the Keck Observatory, made up of two giant telescopes, each with a light-collecting mirror of 10 m (33 feet) across. They can work together to create an even more sensitive star-spotting machine.

The Canada-France-Hawaii telescope on Mauna Kea, in Hawaii.

ASIMO

A lot of today's robots can build cars, play chess, or defuse bombs, but they don't resemble people, as the robots in sci-fi movies do. ASIMO, however, is different. It's the world's most advanced humanoid robot. It can walk, run, dance, climb stairs, serve tea, see, talk, and listen to commands, and it looks spookily alive.

MAKING A HUMANOID

ASIMO is still being developed. The Japanese car company Honda has been building and improving ASIMO models since the 1980s. It's taken lots of technological skill and computer wizardry to give ASIMO the ability to walk like a human and to sense and identify objects using a video camera system.

ROBOTS TO SERVE US

ASIMO is inspired by the sci-fi idea of robots being able to do everyday jobs for humans, interact with us, and even befriend us. In movies, robots are often so advanced, they're treated as normal people. ASIMO hasn't yet reached that stage, but meeting it is a strange experience. Because of its appearance, people can't help responding to it as if it has its own feelings and wishes.

AWESOMENESS

😵 😵 😵 😵

It will take time, but ASIMO is paving the way for a world where household robot companions are a reality.

Honda says that ASIMO is an acronym for Advanced Step in Innovative Mobility.

VITAL STATISTICS ASIMO looks like a small, high-tech astronaut, with a visor-like face and chunky white body. It's 130 cm (51 inches) tall and looks a bit like a child. It doesn't move exactly like a human, but it can run at up to 8 km/h (5 mph).

NANOMACHINES

A nanometer is a unit of measurement that's one billionth of a metre, or one millionth of a millimetre. The term 'nano' is generally used to describe teeny-tiny objects. Scientists are starting to build teeny machines that range from 1 to 100 nanometres across.

TEENY TECH

So far, we've only managed to make a few very basic nanomachines, by arranging individual molecules into particular shapes. One example is a nano car that was developed in 2005. Its wheels are made of ball-shaped carbon molecules, called buckyballs, that can roll so that the car moves around. Scientists hope that one day lots of nanomachines like this can work together to make other machines, or do useful jobs, such as dealing with dangerous waste.

A computer illustration of what nanobots may look like.

NANOROBOTICS

Scientists hope to build nanoscale robots, or 'nanobots'. They could be especially useful in medicine – they might be able to travel inside the body and deliver drugs, or be programmed to find and kill cancer cells or dangerous viruses.

AWESOMENESS

😀 😀 😀 😀 😀

Nanotechnology gives us a glimpse into what could be an awesome science fiction–style future.

A nanorobot modelled on the shape of a spider.

NANO TERROR While nanomachines and nanobots may be very useful, some people are scared they could become a nightmare. What if these microscopic machines began replicating themselves and running out of control? No one yet knows if this could really happen.

ACKNOWLEDGMENTS

Marshall Editions would like to thank the following for their kind permission to reproduce their images.

Key: t = top   b = bottom   c = centre   r = right   l = left

Cover: Shutterstock/David Evison; Shutterstock/Hunor Focze; Virgin Atlantic © 2009 Virgin Galactic, all rights reserved; Shutterstock/Shutterstock/Feraru Nicolae; Sea Pics; Corbis/David Pu'u; Shutterstock/Mirounga

Pages: 1 Getty Images/AFP; 2–3 Getty Images/David Fleetham; 4–5 Science Photo Library/Soames Summerhays; 6–7 Nasa/Dryden Historical Aircraft Photo Collection; 8–9 Alamy/David Olsen; 10 Shutterstock/Galyna Andrushko; 11 Getty Images/G. Brad Lewis; 12 Photolibrary/Christian Heinrich/Imagebroker; 13 Shutterstock/Oleg Kozlov; 14 Photolibrary/Douglas Peebles; 15l Getty Images/Lonely Planet Images/Grant Dixon; 15r Getty Images/Aurora/Andrew Querner; 16t NASA; 16c NOAA; 16b NOAA/Ship Collection; 17t NOAA Ocean Explorer Gallery/Catalina Martinez; 17b Science Photo Library/P Rona/OAR/National Undersea Research Program/NOAA; 18t Sam Meacham CINDAQ/MCEP; 18b Shutterstock/Ostill; 19t Corbis/Hemis/Romain Cintract; 19b Shutterstock/Nickolay Stanev; 20tr Shutterstock/Debra James; 20b Corbis/Theo Allofs; 21 Getty Images/Schafer & Hill; 22 Corbis/Matthieu Paley; 23 Alamy/Blickwinkel; 24 Corbis/Hemis/Patrick Escudero; 25tr Shutterstock/Neo; 25b Alamy/Jack Sullivan; 26tr Photoshot/Oceans Image/Michael Patrick O'Neill; 26b Alamy/Jon Arnold Images; 27t Corbis/Frans Lanting; 27br Corbis; 28 Getty Images/Stockbyte; 29 Shutterstock/LaurensT; 30 Shutterstock/JeremyRichards; 31 Shutterstock/Angels Gate Photography; 32 Getty Images/Speleoresearch & Films/Carsten Peter; 33 FLPA/R Dirscherl; 34 Getty Images; 35tr Photolibrary/Frances Furlong; 35cr&b FLPA/Imagebroker/Marko König; 36 Science Photo Library/Soames Summerhays; 37 The Montserrat Volcano Observatory; 38tl Shutterstock/Ffooter; 38t NASA; 39 Judy Rushing; 40bc Corbis/Gerd Ludwig; 40–41 Shutterstock/Dr. Morley Read; 41 Photoshot/NHPA/David Woodfall; 42l Alamy/Planetpix; 42tr Shutterstock/Ambient Ideas; 43 Ardea/Graham Robertson; 44tl Corbis/Anup Shah; 44tr FLPA/Minden Pictures/Richard Du Toit; 45bl Corbis/Juan Medina; 45tr Shutterstock/Grafvision; 45tl Shutterstock/Tischenko Irina; 46tr Alamy/Ace Stock; 46b Corbis/Visuals Unlimited; 47 Shutterstock; 48 Alamy/A

T Willett; 49tl Corbis/Jim Edds; 49b NOAA; 50 Corbis/TW Photo; 51 Alamy/Unai Peña; 52 Getty Images/Ralph H Wetmore II; 53 Peter Charlesworth; 54 FLPA/Matthias Breiter; 55 Photolibrary/Kathie Atkinson; 56 Alamy/Peter Arnold/Astrofoto; 57 NASA/Image Exchange; 58 Science Photo Library/Mark Garlick; 59 Science Photo Library/Chris Butler; 60 Corbis; 61t Corbis; 61b Corbis/Roger Ressmeyer; 62 Rodrigo da Silva Guerra/Tioguerra/Flickr; 64 Corbis/Latitude/Philippe Body/Hemis; 65 Corbis/Yann Arthus-Bertrand; 66 Alamy/Travelbild; 67l Photolibrary/Aflo Foto Agency/Yoshio Tomii Photo Studio; 67r Corbis/Yann Arthus-Bertrand; 68 Alamy/Hemis/Marc Dozier; 69tr Corbis/Jonathan Blair; 69b Flickr/Christine Whelton/Gardinergirl; 70t Shutterstock/Sandra van der Steen; 70b Alamy/Imagebroker/FB Fischer; 71t Shutterstock/CQ; 71b Bridgeman Art Library/Dinodia; 72t Jacques Rougerie; 72b Reuters; 73 Photolibrary/Brand X Pictures/Steve Allen; 74 Corbis/Danny Lehman; 75t Getty Images/George Rodger; 75b Getty Images/Salvatore Laporta; 76 Alamy/Travelpixs; 77 Corbis/Yann Arthus-Bertrand; 78 Alamy/John Lander; 79 Shutterstock/Jonathan Larsen; 80 Shutterstock/Perkus; 81 Alamy/Picture Contact; 82 Shutterstock/Philip Lange; 83 Photolibrary/Superstock/Kurt Scholz; 84 Corbis/David Frazier; 85 Getty Images/AFP; 86 Alamy/JTB Photo Communications Inc; 87 Corbis/Du Huaju/Xinhua Press; 88 Reuters; 89cl Photolibrary/Chad Ehlers; 89r Corbis/Karen Kasmauski; 90 Niels Haakman, Yantai CIMC Raffles Offshore Ltd; 91 © TAKRAF GmbH, all rights reserved; 92 Photoshot/Andrew Gombert/UPPA; 93t Australian National Maritime, Sydney; 93b Rex Features/Newspix; 94 Auke Visser, Holland; 95 Rex Features; 96 Nasa/Dryden Historical Aircraft Photo Collection; 97t Oleg Belyakov/Airliners.net; 97b Topfoto/RIA Novosti; 98t Corbis/Reuters/Peter van Bastelaar; 98c Royal Navy/Westland Helicopters; 98b Shutterstock; 99t Travis Pictures/Flickr; 99b Reuters; 100t Corbis/Ali Haider/EPA; 100b Alamy/Jakub Michalak; 101 Virgin Atlantic © 2009 Virgin Galactic, all rights reserved; 102 NASA/Jet Propulsion Laboratory; 103t Science Photo Library; 103b NASA/Hubble Space Telescope; 104 NASA/Image Exchange/Kennedy Space Station; 105t NASA; 105b NASA; 106 Corbis/In Pictures/Fritz Hoffmann; 107t Alamy/John Lander; 107b Corbis/Gerd Ludwig; 108bl Photolibrary/Jon Heras; 108br Corbis/EPA/Martial Trezzini; 109 Corbis/David Frazier; 110 Honda; 111t Science Photo Library/Pasieka; 111b Science Photo Library/Animate4.com